Shirley Hardy-Rix & Brian Rix

Since their first motorcycle ride from England to Australia through Europe, the Middle East and Asia, Shirley and Brian have ridden more than 170,000 kilometres through 68 countries over six continents.

Brian retired in 2011 after serving as a policeman in Victoria for 36 years. During that time, he headed up the Homicide Squad, investigated drug trafficking, kidnappings, armed robberies and worked undercover. He spent the final five years of his career as President of the powerful police union, the Police Association.

Shirley met Brian when working as a crime reporter on Melbourne television and radio. She is now a freelance journalist, magazine editor and publicist.

She has published two collections of humorous police stories – *Cops, Crooks and Catastrophes* and *More Cops, Crooks and Catastrophes*. Together she and Brian have written *Two for the Road* about their motorcycle trip from London to Australia and *Circle to Circle* about their ride from the bottom of South America to the very top of North America.

Not all those who wander are lost
J.R.R. Tolkien

For our family and friends
who encourage us to live our dreams

THE LONG WAY TO VLADIVOSTOK

A journey through Scandinavia and the Silk Road to Siberia

Shirley Hardy-Rix
& Brian Rix

Aussies Overland

Published in 2016 by Aussies Overland
www.aussiesoverland.com.au aussiesoverland@hardyrix.com.au

Copyright all text, photos & maps © Shirley Hardy-Rix & Brian Rix 2016

All rights reserved. Without limiting the rights under copyright reserved above, no part of this publication may be reproduced, stored in or introduced into a retrieval system, or transmitted, in any form or by any means (electronic, mechanical, photocopying, recording or otherwise) without the prior written permission of both the copyright owner and the above publisher of this book.

National Library of Australia
Cataloguing-in-Publication entry

Hardy-Rix, Shirley, author. Brian Rix, author
The Long Way to Vladivostok: A journey through Scandinavia and the Silk Road to Siberia

ISBN: 978-0-646-95373-1

Hardy-Rix, Shirley. Rix, Brian. Biography.
Motorcycle touring. Motorcycling. Voyages and world travels.

Design & pre-production by High Horse Books
www.highhorse.com.au
Maps by Laurie Whiddon

Contents

Map of the journey	vi
Norway: Shirley	1
Tajikistan: Brian	2
The Road to Scandinavia	5
Norway	35
Finland and Sweden	63
Western Russia: St Petersburg to Volgograd	85
Kazakhstan	131
Uzbekistan	146
Tajikistan	181
Back into Russia: Kyrgyzstan and Kazakhstan	215
Western Siberia: Barnaul to Ulan Ude	235
Mongolia	260
Eastern Siberia: Ulan Ude to Vladivostok	278
South Korea	297
Acknowledgements	307
Follow our journeys	308

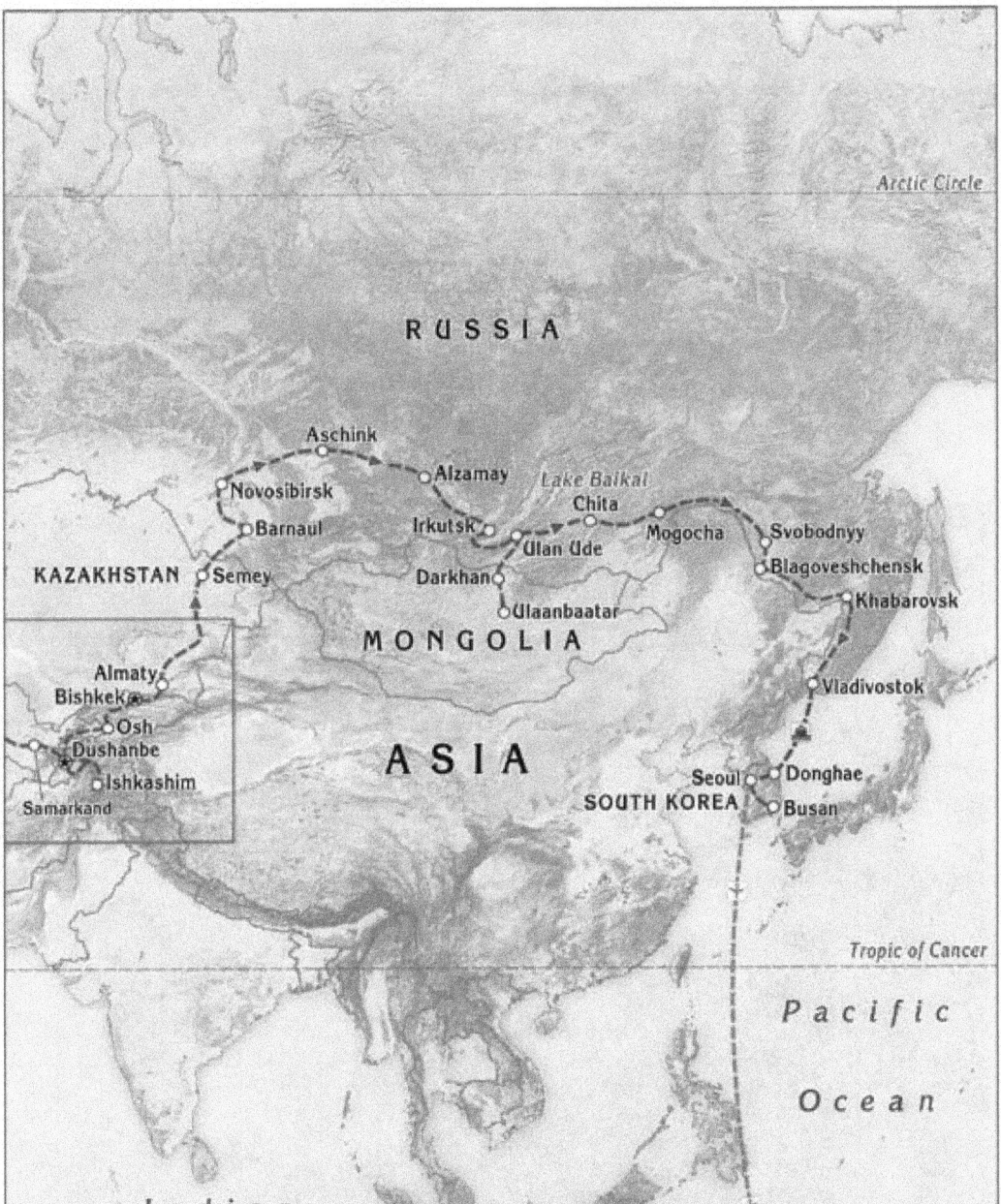

Lysefjordveien, Norway

Norway

June 2015

Shirley: The strong, icy wind is swirling around us, pushing the bike to the very edge of the road. Brian is struggling to keep it on track, wrestling the bike as it moves closer to the cliff edge.

It's only 40 kilometres from the Nordkapp tunnel to Skarsvag, the town at the tip of Europe, but it's a gruelling ride. The cold is biting through our layers of protective gear and our heated vests. I can't feel my feet. The one thing I can feel is my heart beating in my chest. I'm frightened.

I hunker down, trying to use Brian as a windbreak, but one minute it's a headwind, the next it is coming from behind, or from the side.

•

The flags outside our hotel are at risk of being shredded in the wind. There's not a soul to be seen in town, except the reindeer that seem oblivious to the deplorable conditions.

The rain is bucketing down but at least the hotel acts as a windbreak while we unload the gear. Inside I bump into a rider walking around in his long underwear. He clearly wasn't expecting a woman who looks remarkably like a drowned rat to walk through the door.

Tajikistan

September 2015

Brian: The temperature hits 40°C again today. It's slow going on these roads that are more like goat tracks, a real effort getting this heavy bike through the sand drifts. The wind is blowing more sand onto the roadway, making it even deeper. We can't open our helmet visors because the sand is being whipped up, stinging our skin.

Despite my best efforts, I crash into the sand, throwing Shirl off the back, face first into the hot sand.

•

On the far side of the town the road starts to climb away from the river, changing from a sand track to a rocky path. The bike is slipping over the larger stones, unable to get traction on the steep and uneven surface.

The corners are so tight I can't see if any vehicles are coming down the hill. I just hope we don't encounter any locals with their donkeys or goats.

One minute we are rounding a tight left-hand corner and then I lose traction. Down we come again and it's not a soft landing. There's no sand here, just rocks. This is tough going.

What the hell are we thinking?

Big Red clicks over 200,000 ks on the road from Khiva to Bukhara, Uzbekistan

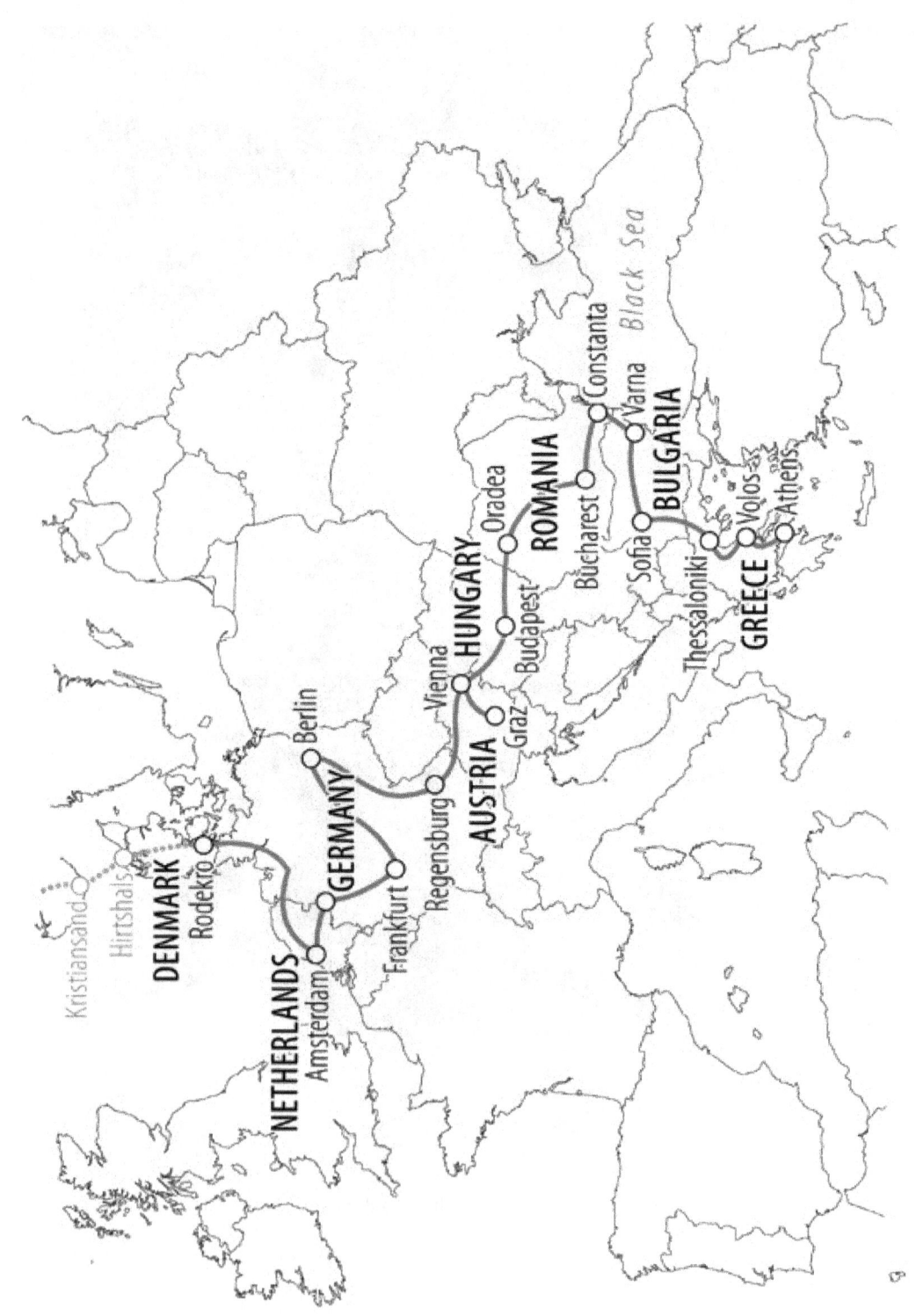

The Road to Scandinavia

4 April – 28 May 2015

Shirley: When Brian came home from lunch with some motorcycle buddies one Friday back in late 2014 and told me he'd booked the motorcycle into a container going to Greece in a few months I was more than a little surprised.

There'd been no real discussions about taking another journey so soon after our 16-month trip through the Americas. We only got home last year!

Brian has always said he was keen to ride across Russia, so – here we go again.

A loose plan is formed to ride from Greece to Norway and then spend some time in Scandinavia before heading into Russia in July with detours into the 'Stans' of Central Asia to explore the old Silk Road. When you say it quickly it doesn't seem too daunting.

•

Getting the motorcycle to Europe is simple, using our friend Dave Milligan's motorcycle freight company, *Get Routed*, to get it to Greece. We'll get visas when we get there and at the border of some of the old Eastern Europe we need to pass through. The rest of the countries all fall under the EU – no visa required.

The preparation for the second half of the ride proves to be complex and time-consuming. Visas for Russia, Uzbekistan, Kazakhstan, Tajikistan and Mongolia have to be obtained before we arrive in those countries. Some of the Central Asian countries also require a letter of introduction. Others don't. We can only apply a few weeks before we arrive and the visas are good for only a month so it's imperative we get the timing right. The upside is we can apply while we're on the road in Europe.

To complicate matters, we have to get our Russian visa before we leave Australia. We need a letter of introduction from a Russian company before we can even apply and can make the application only 45 days before our expected arrival. We also need a business visa rather than a 30-day tourist visa because we will go into Russia three times. It's bamboozling.

With a calendar and maps spread across the kitchen bench and the help of a very patient travel agent in our home city of Melbourne, discussions with other travellers and online research, we manage to sort things out. Timing is crucial as we have to get to Siberia in the summer.

Visas planned, we have to organise insurance for the motorcycle in Europe and the paperwork to get the bike out of and back into Australia. Compulsory third-party insurance is simple – a Green Card will cover us for all of Europe and Russia. Comprehensive insurance for the motorcycle is too expensive to bother with. We opt for a *Carnet de Passage* through the local automobile association, to guarantee we will bring the motorcycle back to Australia, even though most countries we visit don't require it. We're erring on the side of caution.

Brian: It's tough leaving home – the kids, grandchildren, our friends, the dog and the cat, but the timing is right. I expected some resistance, but Shirl embraced the idea pretty quickly and was soon absorbed in guidebooks, making lists of 'must see' places in obscure locations and even trying to master some Russian.

•

Arriving in Greece on April 4 gives us the chance to catch up with Nikos and Judy, two wonderful locals we met back in 2003 when we visited their photographic shop to get some photos we needed for visa applications.

We haven't seen them for more than a decade but they haven't changed a bit. Well, like us, they're a little bit older but their incredibly positive outlook on life is still there and they just want to show us the wonderful side of their homeland.

Over a Hellenic feast of dips, bread, octopus, lamb, salad and dolmades at a local taverna we catch up on their life. The political and financial problems of their homeland are taking their toll but Nikos is a 'glass half full' kind of guy. Their photographic business is slow, but he's sure things will get better later in the year. We hope so, for everyone's sake.

It's wonderful exploring Athens and being with friends but what we really want to see is the bike.

•

When we've organised shipping the motorcycle overseas ourselves the most stressful part has been clearing the bike out of customs at its destination, particularly in Chile back in 2011 when the language difficulties added an extra problem to the normal paperwork difficulties. Using *Get Routed* is a bit more expensive but it's pretty much stress-free.

The bike left Australia back in February, strapped down on a metal cradle inside a shipping container.

Now, eight weeks later, we get a bus to the Athens freight yard, roll the bike out of the container, sign a document organised by the shipping agent and ride to the nearest petrol station to fuel up. Simple.

Let the ride begin.

•

Our first day on the bike and it's raining – terrific! Nikos and Judy are riding with us to Delphi and as we leave the city it's still pissing down and only 6.5°C – cold, wet and windy. This isn't what we expected. Not here. Not in Greece.

It's getting colder as we climb into the mountains. The scenery is amazing. Nikos leads us into a valley that is a snow bowl – white, beautiful and bloody cold; 25cm of snow fell here yesterday.

Little do we know what the weather has in store for us in Scandinavia.

•

Nikos suggests we visit the town of Distomo, about 20 kilometres from Delphi. Back in 1944 more than 200 men, women and children were massacred here by the Nazis in retaliation for an attack on an SS unit they didn't commit.

To get there we ride through Arachova, and it's mayhem on this

Saturday of a long weekend. Two buses come together, nose to nose and the traffic banks up in both directions. The street is so narrow even we can't sneak through. A local shopkeeper comes out and takes over. We sit, patiently watching the street theatre as she gets the buses to back up and give each other a bit of wriggle room. She is definitely the woman in charge.

Shirley: The wind whips around the monument to the innocents of Distomo who were murdered. It is sobering to see the lists of names of the dead. Some were just babies, only weeks or months old. Entire families were butchered. Carved into the stone are images of townsfolk cowering before the armed soldiers.

In a crypt under the marble there is a number of skulls, some clearly show the signs of the bashings handed out. It is an incredibly moving experience and sad, so very sad.

•

Easter Sunday and we're heading back to Arachova for lunch with Nikos' cousin. The patriarch is in his 80s and holds court on the rooftop deck, supervising the cooking of the lamb on the spit. He is propped up on a chair, supporting his gnarly frame with a walking stick. When he speaks the family listens, even though I'm sure they've heard his stories a hundred times before. Using his granddaughters as interpreters, he tells us about his childhood in this town during the Nazi occupation. The soldiers asked him to get a lamb from the fields and kill it for them. He ran into the fields and just kept on running, hiding in neighbouring villages, until the war ended.

The family is very welcoming and include us in all the festivities like close friends, not strangers who don't even speak the language. We crack red-coloured hard-boiled eggs for luck and get to taste the lamb's liver – a special treat offered first to the guests. I love it. Brian isn't so keen but it's the only thing he doesn't enjoy today.

Scenery and towns are a major part of any trip, but it's meeting the locals and being a part of their festivities that's enriching. It's hard saying goodbye to friends, old and new, along the way.

Brian: Before we left home we cut back the amount of stuff we packed, but loading the bike from memory is always tricky. Obviously

Livadia, Greece – we didn't expect snow

Livadia, Greece with Nikos

we didn't cut back enough. Fully loaded the bike is bloody heavy. I've got to reduce the weight, somehow. We've packed the camping gear, mainly for emergencies. I need to think about what we 'really' need and what we can do without. Frankly, it's doing my head in. The poor bike, while not struggling, is sluggish compared to what I know it can do.

•

Our plan is to take the scenic route from Greece through Bulgaria, Romania and Hungary to Vienna where we will be on time to get the first of our essential visas for Central Asia.

•

Heading to Thessaloniki it's a fast run along the foothills of Mount Olympus. It's windy, almost blowing a gale, with a headwind to boot. My neck and shoulders ache from pushing against the buffeting for the last 100 kilometres. Shirl is the same. Finally, we slow down coming into Thessaloniki. The GPS coordinates are taking us straight to the Olympia hotel. The traffic is thick so I don't want to make a navigational mistake. An irate taxi driver yells abuse at me… for going too slow. The blonde-haired woman behind the wheel lets fly with a tirade that obviously includes a fair share of profanities, while gesticulating madly. Shirl lifts the visor on her helmet and gives her a blast back. That's my girl.

•

It's time for our first border crossing, from Greece into Bulgaria, and we don't know what to expect. We always prepare for spending hours going through the paperwork and are pleased if it takes less time.

Leaving Greece, we get a stamp in our passports, a grin from the border guard, and we're on our way. On the far side of no man's land there are two Bulgarian police officers lazing on a seat. I tell them we are Australians on an Australian bike. The older and fatter one waves his hand and says 'you go'. It's the same response at the customs office – a pretty easy border crossing.

The GPS isn't reading our Bulgarian map. I need to fix that before we go too much farther. I pull over and a gypsy man with badly dyed blonde hair, sipping cheap wine from a plastic cup, wants me to pay him to give us directions. Shirl wants to give him money so he'll piss off. I tell her to take her hand out of her pocket. Our little would-be guide is annoyed and abuses me in his native tongue. Tell someone who cares.

•

I have no idea what the open speed limit is. Coming into a town a truck driver flashes me. Sure enough, around the corner is a police car with the radar gun out. I get the eyeball but I'm sure I'm well under the limit. The villages look very poor. Horse-drawn carts are becoming common place. Everything is a bit 'grey' with the larger towns showing signs of their communist past, with massive, soulless concrete apartment blocks. I wonder if life has changed for these people in the years since it became the Republic of Bulgaria and held free elections.

Shirley: We're heading to the Rila Monastery. Brian isn't keen on riding into big cities. He reckons, apart from historic centres, they're all the same. So, instead of riding into Sofia, he's decided we're going to the UNESCO-listed religious community. Once we turn off the main highway the road deteriorates. I wonder if the monastery is going to be worth it.

•

Outside the monastery two Greek men ask us if we are the Australians. They're friends of Nikos and Judy from Athens, holidaying in Bulgaria. It's a small world.

The Rila Monastery is breathtaking – adorned with religious paintings, it's said to be the most impressive Orthodox monastery in all of Eastern Europe. In all the paintings good triumphs over evil, with God defeating the devil with his pointy ears and tail.

Established by a hermit in the 9th Century, Rila is a place of worship in a living museum.

The actual church is surrounded by a three-storey, brightly painted accommodation block with wooden stairways climbing up to the balcony. This is a private area, for the priests only. One of the religious men walks past wearing his long black robes, with his long black hair tied back into a ponytail. The only thing detracting from the image is the plastic shopping bag he is carrying.

It's been worth the terrible ride to get here. Brian was right to bring us here and he has mellowed. Tomorrow we'll ride to Sofia – just for one night - and then to the Bulgarian biker camp he is so keen to visit.

Brian: Shirl's right – I hate big cities but I concede we should explore Sofia, the Bulgarian capital. The pot-holed highway and one-way streets in the city itself don't improve my humour, but walking in the old city centre is something else.

We don't have to walk far. Shirl's picked a hotel right on the edge of the historic centre. We cross the Lion's Bridge over the Vladaya River and find a small restaurant for lunch. There's only salad and beer as the power is off. That's OK. The sun is shining and the beer goes down well.

The massive Alexander Nevsky Cathedral, with its gold-plated domes, is Sofia's best-known tourist attraction. Decorated with onyx, alabaster and Italian marble, it is breathtaking.

The much smaller and less elaborate Russian Church is equally as lovely – in its own way.

We feel very safe walking the streets of Sofia, past mosques and churches, strolling through gardens and just window shopping. We were both a bit anxious about the language difficulties here in Eastern Europe but are pleasantly surprised by the number of people who speak English. Even the woman running a small ice-cream kiosk speaks perfect English. We're embarrassed by our lack of language skills.

•

I have read about the Moto Camp Bulgaria and I'm determined to get there. Shirl thinks it's a bad idea because we haven't been able to raise them on the telephone and they haven't responded to our emails. The owner, Doug, has ridden across Russia on a Harley and I'd like to talk to him about it. He's bound to have some good tips for us.

I convince Shirl it's worth the risk, so, we hit the road.

Taking the main highway out of Sofia is pretty easy, thanks to the GPS. About 190 kilometres out there's a turn-off with a sign to the biker camp, but the GPS is saying to go on farther. It's a little confusing but I put my faith in modern technology, turning into a smaller street where a grader is trying, unsuccessfully, to flatten out the bumps in the road.

Now the GPS is leading us in circles. We cross the highway and

At the Temple of Poseidon, Greece with Nikos and Judy

Rila Monastery, Bulgaria

Sofia Cathedral, Bulgaria

Stone Forest, Romania

Ceausescu's folly – Bucharest, Romania

then double back and end up passing the grader again. I can't help but yell at the inanimate object attached to the bike. It doesn't make any difference, but I feel better. The grader driver does his best to give us directions and we somehow end up in the little village of Idilevo and find the camp. Its iron gates are chained up with a massive padlock, making sure no one can get in. A friendly black Labrador bounds up to see us, his tail wagging, and pokes his nose through the bars for a pat.

A young local girl runs down the hill from a farmhouse and tells us that Doug and his wife have gone to England for a week. Well, that will explain why they're not answering their phone!

Shirley: It's a bloody long ride from here to anywhere, really. It's hot, but we decide to push on. We use the free Wi-Fi at a McDonalds on the highway and check out the hotels in Varna, on the shores of the Black Sea. We find one near the Sea Gardens, presuming this will be easy to find. What we don't realise is that the gardens are actually a huge park running for several kilometres along the Black Sea front. We eventually find the address with the GPS but have trouble finding the hotel itself because of roadworks. It's the little things that can turn a pleasant ride into a stressful excursion.

A meal of delicious local mussels and a glass or two of local wine and all is forgotten. A bad day on the road is over.

•

My bag seems to have a bit of room in it and I'm convinced it's because I've mastered the dark art of pannier bag packing. Sadly, that's not the case. I've managed to leave half my underwear and two of my three T-shirts in the hotel in Sofia. I post my sorry tale on Facebook and my girlfriends rally around with lots of advice on shopping. They always see the bright side!

•

A short distance from town is a forest of 50-million-year-old stone pillars that were once on the seabed. The ride out there takes us along a quieter back road where, every couple of hundred metres, there are young prostitutes waiting to ply their trade with the passing truckies. It's a sad sight. Some of the women are wearing bikini briefs and skimpy tops. Others are just in jeans and T-shirts. They look bored and uninterested, sitting on abandoned tyres smoking cigarettes and drinking Coke.

I have to laugh when I think back to a ride in Spain a few years ago, passing plastic chairs strategically placed along the roadside. I asked one of the locals if they were bus stops. Clearly I am very naïve. They were there to give the working girls a break from standing on their spiked heels!

Brian: The wind is strong and it's cold, just 5°C. This is not what we expect from the Black Sea. Rather than blue and inviting, the sea is black and gloomy. The heated vests we brought with us from Australia may be a bit finicky to connect but the added warmth makes riding in these conditions much easier to handle.

At the Romanian border the official buildings are ramshackle and look as though they've been here since the days of the Soviet Union. Our arrival sparks a lot of interest, with officials shouting to each other to come and check out the Australian motorcycle. We are certainly breaking the boredom of their day.

While our passports are taken into one of the offices we get talking to a Bulgarian bicycle rider who forgot his passport and is waiting for his friends to bring it to him. He's all decked out in Lycra, prepared for a long strenuous ride. I can't help but notice his bike has a numberplate and a registration label. Every time a bicyclist does something wrong in Australia there are calls for bicycles to be registered like cars. The rider is surprised that we are interested. It's just normal procedure in Bulgaria.

Before we can continue the conversation our passports return. A couple of stamps and we are into Romania and on the road to Bucharest and Transylvania.

•

Our hotel in Bucharest has promised secure parking which turns out to be a space on the street, outside the hotel's side door. Shirl is worried. While I try and convince her there's nothing to worry about, I do unload everything, including the bag with all of our camping gear. No point in tempting fate.

•

Our room is on the top floor, with views over the rooftops to the Palace of the Parliament – dictator Nicolea Ceausescu's folly. There's an English language tour of this testament to the excesses of the disgraced dictator this afternoon.

Without thinking, Shirl leaves her heated vest on underneath her jumper and this creates a great deal of interest from the security staff. It sets off the alarms when she walks through the metal detector. You can imagine what they must think of the wires inside the vest. Eventually she convinces them she's just a chilly pillion passenger and not a terrorist.

Ceausescu ordered the demolition of 20 per cent of the city to build this massive structure. Hundreds of homes, churches and historic buildings were destroyed after he gave 40,000 people a day's notice to leave their homes. He didn't care that he was destroying history and leaving thousands of people homeless. His people starved as he spared no expense on the building. Its marble and crystal interior and the works of art, tapestries and sculptures throughout the 1,000 rooms prove, in some cases, that just because you have money you don't necessarily have style.

•

What is left of old Bucharest is fascinating. The domed Bank Palace dominates the cobblestoned streets where the tiny St Stavropoleos Church is a peaceful oasis in the heart of the city. We find the Pasajul Macca, a very narrow, covered shopping street, built in the 1800s to encourage people to shop in bad weather. We dine in a nearby café, trying out the local Mici, a spicy skinless sausage, and Romanian sausages, that come rolled in a coil, held together by skewers. All very tasty.

•

We have only a couple of hundred kilometres to get to Brasov in the heart of Transylvania. It's cold but not raining when we leave. Before long the temperature drops to single figures and we have to stop to put on our winter gloves and the heated vests.

The mountains are shrouded in clouds but it's dry until we get to Sinaia. It's snowing and not just a light dusting of snow like we encountered in Greece, but heavy snow that is settling on the bike's screen and our helmets.

I slow right down. Ice, snow and motorcycles don't mix. The traffic is queuing up behind us and I couldn't care less. Normally this would worry me, but there's no way I'm going to go any faster. At least if we come off it won't be hard or fast!

We weave our way down the other side of the mountain through the snowfall on wet, slippery roads. The ice warning light is on -2.5°C!

Eventually the road flattens out and, while the snow is all around us, it's not actually snowing.

I didn't expect the weather to be this bad in April.

I want to ride the Transfagarasan Highway, said to be one of the world's best roads. It's not far from here, but it's closed because of the ice and snow. Ceausescu built it through the Carpathian Mountains, as an escape route, just in case the Russians decided to invade. We'll have to tackle it another time.

Shirley: I hate rides like today's. It's a relief to get to Brasov and explore the old city on foot. We stroll along the cobblestoned Republic Street to the Black Church and squeeze into the narrowest street in the town. I can stand in the middle and touch the walls of the buildings on each side. The wind is bitterly cold so we hit the Irish Pub (yes, they are everywhere) for a couple of drinks before going to the Romantic restaurant for dinner. It's Romantic by name and by nature. A table for two, a bottle of local wine and some tasty morsels are perfect.

Walking back to our hotel we realise business is obviously slow for some of the local companies. The undertaker is offering 30 percent discounts on coffins, with a very stylish window display of his best.

•

We wake to clear blue skies and sunshine – perfect riding weather for our trip to Bran's Castle – legendary home of Vlad the Impaler and the Dracula myth.

Perched high above the town of Bran in Transylvania, it's easy to envisage Bram Stoker's Dracula prowling the narrow corridors, secret staircases and tiny passageways. Rather than the home of bloodthirsty vampires, the castle was actually the favourite home of the Romanian royal family until they were expelled by the communists in the 1940s.

It's also a good place for me to replace one of my T-shirts now probably being worn by a housemaid in Sofia. Under the castle walls

Working the highways,
Romania

Hungarian goulash,
Budapest,
Hungary

Peles Castle, Sanaia, Romania

Dracula's Bran Castle,
Transylvania,
Romania

are scores of tourist shops all selling the same merchandise – T-shirts, Dracula masks, fake vampire fangs. I pass on the fangs.

•

We take the back roads to Sinaia and Peles Castle. It's a great ride through sunny valleys that two days ago were covered in snow. There's still snow in the shadows on the side of the road but the road itself is clear. Today Brian is a happy man riding through the Carpathian mountain forests on a dry road with barely a car in sight.

This castle is much more modern, with fairytale turrets, towers and a terrace lined with statues, all set amid rolling lawns. Inside is opulent in the extreme. Each ground-floor room is designed in a different European style. The Venetian room has massive Murano glass chandeliers and mirrors. We take a break at the castle's café overlooking the palace and have what is probably the most expensive drink you can get in this part of the world. It's so expensive Brian won't tell me how much he spent! Who cares – you can't take it with you!

•

We cross into Hungary where the paperwork is a little more complicated. Here we need a 'vignette' pass so we can ride on the freeways. It is sold in a small building at the back of the service station just over the border. From here it's only a short run to Budapest and the mighty Danube River.

Our hotel is just a short walk from the Citadel, high above the river. It's the perfect spot to watch the sunset over this magical city under the watchful eyes of the Liberty Statue. Erected by the communists in 1948 to commemorate the end of Nazi occupation, she's quite a lady, standing on a 26-metre pedestal and holding aloft a palm leaf.

•

Cruising the 'Blue' Danube is a must, even though it's not actually very blue. No matter what the colour of the water the views of the city from this perspective are terrific. We sail past the impressive parliament building, the castle, the churches and under historic bridges. After a feast of Hungarian goulash served in a hollowed-out cob loaf of bread and washed down with a beer in an outdoor market, we wander the streets, visiting the majestic St Stephen's Basilica and the Fisherman's

Bastion with its ornate turrets and nooks and crannies overlooking the city. We fall in love with Budapest. For us, it's right up there with Paris, Barcelona and Zaragoza as one of our favourite cities.

Brian: We leave Eastern Europe behind and ride to Vienna in perfect time to get the first of the visas we need for Central Asia. We got our Russian visa in Australia. Here we'll get the Tajikistan visa and, hopefully, the special permit we need to visit the autonomous Pamir region that borders Afghanistan. Foreigners can only visit with the permission of the government.

It should be a simple process. We know that we need to pay the fees for the visas into the Tajikistan bank account in any branch of the local Uni Credit bank. Armed with a map from our hotel we walk the streets of the city and find every other bank, but not Uni Credit.

Shirl disappears into a hotel in the heart of the city and gets another map and more directions. She strides off, exuding confidence. When she gets to the corner where our bank should be there's another bank there. I'm starting to get a little testy.

Shirley: That is a major understatement.

Brian: Shirl goes into the bank to ask directions and comes out looking very smug. This is the bank, even though it's not. Apparently we can deposit into the Uni Credit accounts at any bank. After all the stress it takes only a few minutes and we've paid our 160 Euro and have our receipt.

Outside the bank there are men in powdered wigs, wearing brocade top coats and breeches, selling tickets to Mozart and Strauss concerts. It's our wedding anniversary tomorrow so I buy tickets for dinner and a show to celebrate the occasion. Shirl forgives me for getting so shitty when we couldn't find the bank.

•

Armed with passports, photos, application forms and our bank receipt we go to the Tajikistan Embassy in an apartment building in the city. It's also not that easy to find. There's only a small flag flying from a first-floor window and a brass plaque on the doorway to indicate we are about to enter Tajikistan territory.

The Danube, Budapest, Hungary

The Hungarian Parliament on the Danube River, Budapest, Hungary

The consular official ushers us into an office where an enormous tapestry of the likeness of Tajikistan President Emomali Rahmon looks down on us. We're going to get to know his face very well in the months ahead.

There's no problem with our application for the visas or the permits to visit the Pamir region, but there will be a delay because the Ambassador has gone home to celebrate May Day. We'll need to come back next week to collect our passports. Luckily, that fits our schedule.

Shirley: Our wedding anniversary treat is a delight. We dine on a traditional meal of soup with shredded pancakes, schnitzel and potatoes and strudel with cream, then go to the Kursalon on the edge of Vienna's city park. Built in the 1800s, Johann Strauss played here. We sit on gold-embossed chairs under enormous chandeliers and listen to the music of Strauss and Mozart, with a little ballet performance thrown in. It might not be everyone's idea of an evening's entertainment but we love it. Happy anniversary, Brian. Twenty-six years down and plenty more to come.

•

Reunited with our passports we head into Germany to catch up with friends and to get our Uzbekistan and Kazakhstan visas. The paperwork for Uzbekistan is a little complicated. We have a letter of introduction organised through our agent in Australia and need to take colour copies of our passports and the application forms to the Embassy in Berlin. Before we can do that we have to deposit money into the Embassy bank account. Luckily there is a Deutsche Bank on just about every corner so we don't have the same stress we had in Vienna.

•

The embassy is surrounded by a metal and brick fence with a very cute, larger than life 'Berlin Bear' statue decorated in an Uzbek theme in the front garden.

The *Konsulat* is just inside the gate and we go in feeling a little trepidation. We've been told the Uzbekistan officials can be difficult and even though we have the letter of introduction we won't automatically get the visas. If they do decide to give us our visas we may have to wait for days for them to complete the paperwork. Hope not.

Behind the counter is a tall, dour-looking man. We explain we want to apply for a visa. He nods at us, stretches out his massive hand and takes our paperwork. He staples it all together and tells us to come back in two days.

'Tomorrow we are closed. It is Victory Day. It is a holiday. Come back Friday.'

That's it. No smile. No chat. Nothing. We will wait while the Uzbek officials celebrate the end of World War II.

•

Berlin is a vibrant city and despite being just about bombed out of existence during the war there's still plenty of history to enjoy. We visit Charlottenburg Palace which has been reconstructed in the decades following the war. In a park alongside one of Berlin's many canals we find a statue of the fathers of Communism – Marx and Engels. Now, this we didn't expect.

•

We have one more visa to get in Germany – Kazakhstan – which we can get in Frankfurt. But, we figure we have time and that paperwork can wait for a few days while we visit with our friends, Bernd and Heidi, whom we met in 2003 in Iran.

Brian: Bernd is like a brother to me and it's great to be with him and Heidi. We ride together through the forests around their town, Kallmerode, in the old East Germany, through small rural communities and on narrow back roads through little villages. At the geographic centre of Germany, we take photos. We're loving being together but our time here is short. We have to get to Frankfurt for our visas and then move on to Scandinavia.

Saying goodbye is always hard. There are tears shed when we bid our friends farewell. We'll see them again – somewhere in this wonderful world.

•

The vivacious Tonya Stevens and her husband, André Haermeyer, a former Victorian politician, have made the country of his birth their home. Tonya has checked out the Kazakhstan consulate for us and downloaded the forms we need. They are in German and Russian – not English, so Tonya's multi-lingual skills come in very handy. André even transfers the visa fees from his online banks. They are making the whole process easier for us.

•

With Tonya as our guide and interpreter we get the train into the suburbs of Frankfurt and walk to the Kazakhstan Embassy. Tonya is ready to speak to the officials in German but they all speak English. It takes only 15 minutes and we're told to come back in a week. It's not ideal but it's not so bad.

•

We head to Bogel, a short ride along the Rhine River from Frankfurt, to visit Jens and Kati, another couple of travellers we met in South America back in 2011, and American Dave Hand. We met Dave in North America in 2012 and rode with him to the Prudhoe Bay, the northern most tip of Alaska.

When we started planning this trip Shirl was conversing with Dave on the Internet. He was planning on being in Europe at the same time as us so it was decided we'd travel together for part of the journey. There seemed to be some synchronicity in riding to the top of Europe, Nordkapp, together. After all, we rode to the top of America together.

Shirley: Jens and Kati are living in a lovely cottage on the edge of the forest high above the Lorelei on the Rhine River. Sitting in the cottage garden under the wisteria in the springtime twilight it's quite a reunion. It begins with a bottle of Black Forest Schnapps and ends with Jens, Dave and Brian practising the difficult art of Mongolian throat singing, preparing us for what lies ahead in that part of the world. Suffice to say it's much quieter when we get up for breakfast.

•

Back in Frankfurt our passports are waiting at the Kazak consulate, stamped with the double entry visas we need. We're set for Central Asia, apart from Kyrgyzstan that will be issued at the border and Mongolia, that we plan to get in Ulan Ude, Russia. Everything is going as planned.

Relaxing at Boppard, Rhine River Germany with Jens, Kati and Dave
The middle of Germany with Bernd, Heidi and Simon Herzberg

Marx & Engels, Berlin, Germany

Brian and Bernd, Kallmerode, Germany

Brian with André and Tonya, Frankfurt, Germany

Some of this trip will be challenging in the extreme. Mongolia has three roads in – one with plenty of sandy tracks, another with multiple river crossings from the west and the main sealed highway from Ulan Ude to the capital Ulaanbaatar. Initially Brian was keen to tackle the roads through western Mongolia but now seems to be leaning towards going in from the north. I'm pretty happy about that, I have to say. Brian says there's no point in killing the bike or us and I'm not going to disagree.

•

This trip back to Frankfurt gives us a chance to send some things home – things we thought we couldn't live without and now realise we can't travel with. I don't know what we were thinking when we packed our collapsible chairs, triple cooking pots and other extraneous items. Add to this some souvenirs and we post just over 10 kilos. Bloody hell! Hopefully getting that off the bike will make a difference.

Brian: We've settled into life in Germany, but it's time to move on. Dave takes the lead on the back roads through forests, past fields of rape and wheat, through tiny villages and past castles, perched high above the river.

After the autobahns we've been riding to get from city to city in Germany the smaller roads are a delight. We're not travelling too fast and there aren't too many trucks. The sun is shining. The roads are good. This is just about perfect riding.

•

We have an appointment to get the bike serviced in Denmark in a few days so there's time for some sightseeing on the way. I know Shirl loves this and Dave is just happy to go with the flow.

Shirley: Organising the accommodation is always my job. When we first started travelling back in 2003 I would let Brian check out the rooms, until I worked out that what he thinks is a suitable room doesn't always match my idea of a suitable room.

At a hotel in Gronau, near the border with the Netherlands, I press the buzzer at the front door – nothing. I walk around the back and can't find any obvious entrance or any signs of life. Then a man appears, looking a little surprised to find me at his door. Using my best German I ask him about rooms. He seems to be telling me this is a private house and the hotel is actually around the corner. Oops.

We find the hotel and the reception is in the bar. The barmaid doesn't speak any English, yet I manage to get a room for us and one for Dave, with breakfast included, and even the code for the Wi-Fi. I'm quite proud of myself.

All those years studying German at Manly Girls' High weren't wasted after all. Miss King would be proud…or maybe not.

•

We take the train from our hotel into the heart of Amsterdam. We emerge from the subway into a seething mass of humanity. There are trams, buses and cars clogging the roads. Cyclists are hurtling along the dedicated bike paths at breakneck speed. People are walking, dodging all of the traffic while others sit in cafés enjoying a drink and watching the madness go by.

It is much more peaceful on the canal boat tour. I just love seeing a city from the water and Amsterdam is an obvious place to take a cruise. We float by skinny houses, big houses, canal boat houses, past the seven bridges, the skinny bridge, Anne Frank's house where the queue goes around the corner, the largest church in town, beautiful bridges and plain bridges – it's a delight.

A walk through the red-light district reveals the working women in the windows. They are young, pretty and uninterested. Many are smoking cigarettes or chewing gum, they're on their phones or just drinking coffee, like the women in Spain and Bulgaria - It's the same the world over. I guess it's a living.

•

Tulip season is over but you can buy bulbs to post home or a cannabis starter kit at the flower market. Cannabis and hash lollies are on sale everywhere. Sitting on a bench overlooking a canal we spot a couple who look as though they are trapped in the 1960s. They're enjoying a joint and it doesn't look as though it's their first for the day.

•

We'd hoped to see fields of tulips but we're not leaving the Netherlands without seeing dykes and windmills. On our way to Denmark we ride to Zaanse Shans, a collection of historic windmills. It's a bit touristy but then we are tourists! The working windmills are scattered along a canal. Some have little shops selling local produce and souvenirs. Others are museums.

The Netherlands really is flat, incredibly flat. The road to Denmark takes us along the Afsluitdijk. At 32 kilometres it's the country's longest dyke. It is one hell of an engineering feat.

Brian: Last year Shirl and I were at a Horizons Unlimited meeting of motorcycle travellers in Queensland and met Erik, a Dane now living in Australia. He has introduced us to his friend Jorgen, a retired BMW mechanic who is happy to come out of retirement to help travellers.

While the bike was in the crate heading to Greece, BMW issued a recall on the rear flange. BMW Germany couldn't help us until August but Jorgen has organised for his local BMW dealer to check out the bike, then we can go to his house for the bike service. Jorgen has mentioned putting us up at his home but we don't want to impose. We'll just get the bike serviced and hit the road.

•

At Toftlund MC, the BMW dealer near Jorgen's home in Over Jestal, the mechanic is expecting us. In half an hour he's checked out the bike, replaced the flange and given it a clean bill of health.

Jorgen has just turned 60 and is making the most of the freedom of retirement by spending plenty of time on the road. We're lucky to catch him at home. His good nature is surpassed only by his generosity.

The first thing he does is show us the rooms he's set up for us. A double for me and Shirl and the smaller room for Dave. He won't accept any arguments. We're staying the night and that is that.

Servicing bikes is Jorgen's hobby. We spend the afternoon in his spotlessly clean workshop talking motorbikes and Scandinavian roads.

Over dinner with his wife, Connie, it's decided we'll have to stay another night so we can go riding tomorrow and then head to Norway the day after.

•

It's flat but every country has its drawcard and in this part of Denmark

On the beach with Dave, Denmark

Dave and Brian at Zaanse Shans, Netherlands

it's the beaches. It's cold but sunny – a pretty good day for a ride.

We head through the flatlands, past more pastures and crops and then we hit the beach. The sand near the road is really soft, churned up by the cars and motorhomes. It's a bit tricky ploughing through this section but once we're on the hard-packed sand it's perfect.

Next stop is Ribe, Denmark's oldest town, existing since the Viking era. We walk along the narrow streets with buildings dating back to the 1600s and earlier. The walls bow out and the roof lines have dropped. It's really quite lovely. The old post office is now a café and perfect spot for lunch. We can't get over how dear Europe is. Just sandwiches cost $100AUD for the five of us! Denmark is the most expensive country we've visited so far.

•

Tomorrow we leave for Norway and begin our assault on Nordkapp – the most northern point of Europe.

Jorgen keeps saying he'd like to come with us.

'No way,' says Connie!

Norway

28 May - 12 June 2014

Shirley: Take the bridge.
Take the ferry.
Everyone has their own idea on how we should get from Denmark to the rest of Scandinavia. I want to take the bridge. First there's a four-kilometre tunnel and then, when you hit the surface, an eight-kilometre bridge linking Denmark to Sweden. I reckon this will be quite dramatic and a once-in-a-lifetime experience.

Jorgen is talking up the ferry. That will take us right into the heart of the fjord country of Norway.

The bridge/tunnel option will mean hours of freeway riding from Sweden to Norway. I still think it's worth it.

Brian and Dave don't agree. The riders have it. We'll take the ferry.

•

It's a three-hour ride from Jorgen and Connie's to the ferry so we have to leave early. You wouldn't think it is spring. It's raining, cold and bleak. We push on for an hour but then we have to stop at a service station to thaw out. I knew I should have put the heated vest on under my riding jacket.

By the time we get to the port at Hirtshals it's stopped raining, which is just as well as we have to queue up in an open yard before we can board the ferry. In two hours we are disembarking at Kristiansand, Norway. I'm pretty paranoid about sea trips but this one is calm and we all manage to catch up on a bit of sleep.

Brian: While Shirl and Dave are snoozing I go into the toilets to find a biker standing in his soaking wet, long johns. He's trying to dry off under the hot-air hand dryer. I noticed him and his mates when we rode onto the ferry. They're riding Harley look-alikes with metal tractor seats and wearing old German World War II helmets and no weather-proof clothing. I wonder how'll they'll survive if they are heading north.

•

Jorgen has booked us into a cabin right on the edge of a fjord at Trysnes Marina. It's just a short ride from the ferry port at Kristiansand. The weather hasn't changed from Denmark's, but what a difference in scenery. After the flat landscape, Norway is breathtaking. The road takes us past lakes, fjords and between rocky outcrops. One thing Dave and I have to remember is the top speed limit here is only 80 kilometres per hour. I don't think that will be a problem. If our first day on the road is anything to go by there will be plenty to look at along the way, so the slower the better.

The scenery is awesome. There's lots of oohing and ahing coming from the pillion in a million. We're both glad the ferry won over the bridge!

•

Our cabin is indeed right on the water's edge. Shirl is organising drinks to take out onto the deck to enjoy the view when there's a knock on the door and before we can say anything, it bursts open. A tall, man armed with maps and guidebooks introduces himself, extending a very weather-beaten hand. He is Frank, a local diver who organises scuba and fishing trips. He's not trying to sell us a tour, he just wants to share his local knowledge.

One place he recommends is Pulpit Rock, a 600-metre sheer rock face above Lysefjord. Shirl doesn't look all that impressed with discussions of hiking to the top. The views would be amazing, I'm sure, but I'm also sure I won't get her up there!

Shirley: Dave is just about the perfect travelling companion. His sense of humour lightens even the dullest moments on the road. His easy-going attitude means there's never an argument about what we should do or where we should stay. If we are happy, he is happy.

His naturally ebullient personality sees him chatting to the locals at every opportunity. If we can't see him, we know he'll be getting to know a stranger or making the most of any free Wi-Fi connection,

Atlantic Highway

Reindeer on the road to Tromso

Lysefjordveien, snow canyons

keeping in touch with one of his many friends at home in Florida.

•

What a beautiful morning. It's sunny and the water is glistening like diamonds and we're all tempted to chill out here and enjoy the view, but the roads are calling.

Of course the sunshine doesn't last. The weather is very changeable up here. It's not long before the clouds move in and the rain comes. It passes and then the hail comes. And it's cold – bloody cold.

•

Dave and Brian have our route planned out so I just get on the back and enjoy the ride. I've checked out lots photos of Norway but they don't prepare me for the superb scenery and impressive roads. It doesn't matter if we are on a tiny back road or a major highway, around every corner the views take my breath away. A 'wow' factor at every turn.

We ride out of the bad weather and stop at a little shop that has a local map on the wall. We are in deep discussion about a road to a viewpoint over the fjord when a man interrupts us. 'Are you lost,' he asks in perfect English. Everyone here speaks English. More shame on us for not knowing at least one other language.

It's hard to explain that we are not lost, well not really. We're looking for a road that comes highly recommended.

He points to a road and tells us to take it. It's a small side road into the mountains and it ends at Pulpit Rock – it's the road we've been looking for – Lysefjordveien.

As we get onto the bike I have one last question. 'Is there snow up there?'

'Oh, yes,' he replies. 'There is snow.'

Brian: He wasn't exaggerating. In a couple of kilometres, we find ourselves in a dreamland of snow, snow and more snow.

The road twists its way through snow piled more than four metres on each side. Beyond the road there is pristine white snow as far as the eye can see. There are snow drifts in the valley that must be metres deep. It is one of the most beautiful sights I've ever seen. All I can hear is Shirl oohing and aahing at every turn. The sun is shining and that makes it even more beautiful, if that is possible.

The road is as clean as a whistle and Dave and I get into the groove of the ride. There's no ice, no gravel, just clean tarmac. It's magic. It is narrow though – just wide enough for two cars to pass so there's not a lot of room for error. It's not a fast ride, but it is brilliant.

We pull off the road at a strategically placed siding and go crazy with the camera and muck around in the snowmaking standing up snow angels and throwing the odd snowball. We are like schoolkids. Dave is from Daytona Beach, Florida. We are from Melbourne, Australia. None of us has ever seen snow like this before.

We dawdle around for about an hour and while we're deciding if we should keep going to Pulpit Rock a huge black cloud looms over the mountains. The weather is closing in. That makes the decision for us. We can see it coming, so we head back the way we came.

The weather catches up with us in a few minutes and we're in a white-out with cloud or fog or both all around us. Dave and I slow right down. This isn't the time for stupidity. We have no idea if there is any traffic coming up the road.

The temperature has dropped to just 1°C and the ice warning light is flashing. There is nothing nice about ice when you're on two wheels and it's even less appealing in a white-out.

The cold and snow are so much easier to deal with than the rain. With the cold and snow, when you start to descend, the weather usually improves and it warms up. Today it's dashed up to 4 - 5°C in no time. With the warmer temperatures comes the rain. When it's raining, there is no getting away from it – it's just wet.

•

We can't shake the rain so it's probably a good time to call it a day. The hotel is expensive - about 1450 Norwegian Kroni, that is more than AUD$200. I am staggered by how expensive everything is up here. Even petrol is more than AUD$2.50 a litre, nearly double what we pay at home.

We think it will be easier if we get some drinks to have in our room rather than buying a drink in a bar at the end of the day. This isn't as easy as it sounds. There's plenty of beer and cider in the local supermarkets but wine and spirits are on sale only at the *Vinmonopolets*, the government-owned alcohol stores. And they aren't on every corner. Some smaller towns don't have one at all. In future we'll have to plan ahead.

Lysefjordveien, snow canyons

Happiness is a good road in the snow

Shirley: It's rained all night and it's cold again this morning. Where is spring?

Going on Jorgen and Frank's advice we ride through Hardangervidda National Park which takes us back up into the mountains. Mountains mean snow and it is divine. I am in love with Norway and will forgive her the cold winds, rain, hail, sleet and snow because of her beauty.
The country is linked by a network of tunnels, ferries and bridges. The paper map shows a turn we need to take. What we don't realise is that the turn is in the middle of a tunnel! Yep, there's a roundabout in the centre of the tunnel. The wrong turn is easy to rectify – Brian and Dave just do another lap around the roundabout, take the right road and then take the bridge over another fjord. It is easy to get befuddled.

After crossing the bridge, the road leads us to another fjord and another ferry crossing. We're getting used to these. The GPS tells us to 'board ferry'. Two of the deckhands, Odin and Andreas, are intrigued by the bikes laden with luggage and foreign number plates. Chatting as we cross the fjord, they give us a geography lesson. We are crossing the Sognefjord, Norway's deepest and longest fjord. It's hard to imagine, but this fjord is 1.5 kilometres deep and stretches for more than 200 kilometres.

•

Checking in to a hotel in Sogndal on the edge of the fjord I notice a really bad smell and I think it's me. Dave can smell it too, but Brian, who has no sense of smell, is oblivious. Lucky him. Dave reckons an animal transport in front of us in one of the tunnels had excrement leaking out of it. We've ridden through it and it's splashed onto my boots, waterproof pants and my jacket. Yuk. My first job tonight is to wash off the shit.

•

It's now the last day in May and still no sign of spring, let alone summer, in Norway. At least it's not raining today, good weather for doing some exploring.

Jorgen told us about the Blaskavan Mountain Road that he says is a much more picturesque way to get to Geiranger Fjord than taking the tunnel. The only problem for us is the road is still closed, because of the winter snow.

That doesn't deter Dave. He heads off up the mountain road with its tight switchback corners and Brian follows. I have no option. Where Brian goes, I go.

The road is narrow and the corners are tight as it passes farms that seem to be deserted apart from the sheep that are wandering across and along the road. They're pretty stupid, trying to outrun the bikes rather than just going back into the paddocks.

Halfway up we are blocked by a barrier. From here the snow is everywhere and it seems to be incredibly deep. No wonder the road is still closed.

Brian: The tunnel the mountain pass avoids is Norway's longest. It runs for 24.5 kilometres. We don't need to travel through it but we should take a look at this feat of modern engineering. The Norwegians obviously expect visitors to just want to take a look. A few kilometres in there is an area where we can pull over, take a few photos and then do a U-turn and ride out again.

This little detour has let the bad weather catch up with us again. Welcome back to the cold, the wind and the rain.

•

We leave the rain behind when we climb into another national park in the mountains. Now it's snowing - again. I have to take the corners a little slower but this does let me enjoy the scenery just as much as Shirl on the back.

The GPS tells me there's a lake alongside the road. Not today. It's obviously frozen and covered in metres of snow. It looks like just another snow field.

•

Dave tells us it's time for a snack. We pull into the town of Lom and find a local produce store. Lunch is off but when Dave turns on his charm the women put together a tasting platter of local cheeses and sausage, washed down with a glass of the local white wine. Now this is the life!

•

Back on the road we take the Dalsnibba Pass to Geiringer Fjord. At the top of the pass the snow is coming down but once we move into the valley we leave the snow behind and the road opens up with switchback after switchback.

Lysefjordveien, snow canyons

Lysefjordveien

Dalsnibba Pass

We are high up in the mountains and below us is the Geiringer Fjord, one of Norway's most beautiful. It snakes its way along the mountain valley floor. It's hard to believe but the scenery just gets better and better.

Shirley: Brian has been looking for a cheaper form of accommodation and we find it in the hills above Geiringer – a two-bedroom cabin. It's right alongside a waterfall that rushes through the property before plummeting into the fjord below. It's impossible to hold a conversation beside it but the little balcony at the front of the cabin is quieter and a pleasant spot for a drink overlooking the town below.

The bedrooms in the cabin have blackout curtains, very necessary up here during the long days of the midnight sun. That hasn't been the case in every hotel. Some have just had thin curtains, making sleep difficult sometimes. It's a weird feeling to look out the window and see broad daylight, knowing it's the wee small hours of the morning when your brain knows it should be dark.

•

We wake to fog over the fjord. It's not a good morning for riding so we decide to take a boat trip on the fjord, that is protected by UNESCO. There are some massive waterfalls crashing down from the mountains to the water. The Seven Sisters, Bridal Veil and the Suitor cover the mountainside in a thin mist. Mother nature has been working overtime here.

This area used to be home to farming families, eking out a living on pastures perched high above the fjord. There are some amazing stories from the late 1800s and early 1900s – like the family who had to tie their children to trees when they were out working the fields so the children wouldn't walk off the edge of the farm and fall to their death. There was another family that had been avoiding the tax collector by hauling up the ladders that were the only way to reach the farm from the water. Another woman raised a family of 10 children at one of these farms, each one born on the farm. They must have been tough people. The government preserves this area, hence its UNESCO listing. What a place!

•

The Norwegian authorities seem to understand the tourist, so when they design a tourist road they create a piece of tarmac with flair and style – like the Atlantic Ocean Road. This eight-kilometre road sweeps along the coastline. In bad weather the waves crash across the road. In good weather it's a dream ride.

It's cold when we head out, of course. We take the inland route and the countryside is incredible but then we get to the coast and there is the road – a sweeping 'wave' over the water.

On one side is the water, on the other are the islands that dot the coast. The water is calm and the traffic light. It's perfect. We ride over the main bridge. And then we ride back. And then we ride over and back again. Like our first ride through Lysefjordveien we just can't believe the beauty and the thought that has gone into creating this motorcycle nirvana. It's only a short piece of road but it's so much fun.

Riding across I do a double take when I look across the islands. There is a long, slim Viking ship moving slowly across the water. It's not a ghost ship, of course. It's a tourist attraction – row your own Viking longship.

•

It's time for a day off the bike and Trondheim is the perfect spot. It's an historic town, dating back to the Viking era, and was the country's capital until the mid-1200s. There are some fascinating architectural masterpieces, like the 11th Century Nidaros Cathedral, where the gargoyles play the violin and carry baskets loaded up with severed heads. There's a bridge built in 1681 that joins the old part of the city with the more 'modern' section. The old warehouses, built on stilts along the river, have been converted into trendy homes and restaurants. It's cold, damp and grey but Trondheim is a sea of colour. Every park and the small gardens are filled with tulips. The tulip season might have been over when we were in Amsterdam but it is in full swing here in the far north.

The Archbishops Palace is now home to Norway's armoury museum that includes a fascinating exhibition dedicated to the Norwegian resistance. It follows the country's military history from the 900s, when every farm had to provide a fully equipped soldier, to the World War II resistance against the German invaders. While the resistance movement was strong, more than 20,000 Norwegians volunteered to fight with the Germans. Some of these traitors infiltrated the resistance, putting

Fish drying, Henningsvær, Lofoten Islands

Henningsvær, Lofoten Islands

Amazing scenery on the road from Bodo to Narvik

the members and their activities at risk. Because of this, many British troops were air-lifted in to carry out sabotage operations. Trondheim has been just the spot for a break from the road.

Brian: Every day we are heading farther north, towards our ultimate destination in Scandinavia – North Cape or Nordkapp, the northernmost road in Europe.

Before we can get to Nordkapp we have to cross the Arctic circle – 66.33.33° N.

It's raining and there is no surprise when the ice warning light comes on as we ride into the mountains. The rain is turning into ice on our visors by the time we get to the Polar Arctic Centre, a shop and café in the middle of a windswept, icy plain. In the few minutes it takes us to find parks for the bikes that ice is now snow. A path has been cleared through the snow from the carpark to the front door. The back door of the centre is blocked by snow drifts that are as a high as the roofline. In the middle of the snowfield behind the centre is the monument that marks the Arctic Circle.

Shirl strides off, determined to get to the monument despite the snow. Dave and I follow, all three of us trying to walk where others have gone before us. The snow's a bit harder-packed there and it's less likely we'll end up to our knees in the stuff.

There is no underestimating this amazing achievement. We're an incredibly long way from home. Back in 2012 we crossed the Arctic Circle in Alaska with Dave. Now, here we are crossing it together again. In Alaska there wasn't much but oil camps above the Arctic Circle, but from here to Nordkapp there are major cities. Life seems goes on as normal in the heart of the land of the midnight sun.

•

What a difference a day makes. We wake to sunshine over the fjord outside our room. It's cold but not cold enough for the waterproof jackets or pants. The sun is shining, the sky is blue and the snow is pristine white – what a day.

We turn a corner and the sun is shining on the snow and the water creating the most glorious reflection in the still waters of the fjord. We pull into a little beach to take photos of this magnificent sight and are joined by three young German soldiers who are taking part in joint manoeuvres in the area. They've been studying the weather patterns and assure us the good weather won't last. Thanks for the good news.

•

At today's lunch stop we meet Gaute, a young Ducati rider who is making his way back to his home in Tromso after getting his bike serviced in Trondheim – a two-day ride. I think he's probably the only Ducati rider in this country – well, he's the first we've seen anyway.
In passing conversation, we mention where we are going to spend tonight in Narvik.

There is more mind-blowing scenery today. It seems like around every corner there is something amazing to see. Tiny cottages in green pastures, small fishing cabins on the edge of the fjords, little towns.

On another ferry crossing another fjord we meet two old Germans who are towing small caravans behind ancient tractors. They are on their way to Nordkapp and plan to get there for mid-summer on June 20. That will be quite an achievement.

The tractors are single seaters and both men complain to Shirl that their wives won't travel with them. I can't imagine I'd be able to convince Shirl to join me for a slow journey on a tractor travelling around 10 kilometres per hour, where the passenger must sit with her back to the driver, with the only view being the caravan they are towing.

Shirley: We ride into the hotel carpark and spot Gaute's Ducati. Tonight is a night for a celebration. Back in 2012 when we crossed the Arctic Circle Dave produced a bottle of Crown Royal Canadian whisky to toast our success. He's been carrying another bottle with him to crack open when we cross the Arctic Circle again. Well, we've done it. We sit around a small table in the parking area at the front of the hotel listening to a local band rehearse in the community hall and sip on whisky. Gaute joins us – even though he can't see why crossing the Arctic Circle is such a big deal. He was born and raised above it and is now raising his own family in Tromso – more than 500 kilometres north of the Arctic Circle.

•

Over breakfast we meet a Spanish rider who is on his way back from Nordkapp. He tells us it is the worst ride he has ever done – cold, wet and windy. Now that's something to look forward to!

Nidaros Cathedral, Trondheim

Trondheim

Road to Nordkapp

Everyone has told us how beautiful the Lofoten Islands are. They haven't been exaggerating. Rocky cliffs surround the fjords, with tiny inlets leading to fishing villages nestled in the backwaters. It is gorgeous. We ride into Henningsvær and find a town surrounded by massive drying racks. Fish bodies are draped over some. Fish heads over others. It smells fishy but not overpowering. Thank goodness it's not hot, even though the climate is milder here because of the Gulf Stream.

Our hotel is next to the fish factory and the owner is very proud to tell us that there's a special on for dinner tonight – whale steak… straight off the whaling ship. I think he's a little offended when I decline this suggestion for the evening meal. I guess Norwegians don't understand, or may not even know about, Australia's opposition to whale hunting.

•

There are two ways for us to get to Tromso. The route that incorporates the ferries will probably take 10 hours. The other is the main road which will mean about six hours of riding. While there's no need to worry about running out of light here, the sun hasn't set for days and won't set for weeks to come, we opt for the shorter ride. One thing about Norway – it doesn't matter which road you take there is always something to see and some scenery to delight you.

Dave takes us over a few back roads. On one we see a mobile home parked at an odd angle. The people are watching a few reindeer grazing on pastures at the edge of the fjord. I encourage Brian to do a U-turn and let me off. I walk down a track, clamber over a chain that is blocking the track and walk on a bit farther until I can get a good look at the family of four. They watch me for a while and then lose interest. I get some great photos of what I presume is a rare sighting of these magnificent creatures we know so much about because of their connection with Santa.

•

In Tromso I finally find a *Vinmonopolet* wine store. I've tried in most of the cities we've visited but I've either been unable to find the store or get there when it is closed. I replenish Dave's whisky and buy a bottle of wine for a special dinner date. We're going to Gaute's tonight for a traditional Norwegian meal. I do hope it's not reindeer.

•

Gaute, his wife Kirstin and their young daughters, Sigrid and Frida, welcome us into their home. The little girls are learning English at school and show off their skills by telling us the English words for things on the table, such as glass and plate. The fun of this wears off pretty quickly. Sigrid leans over and says to her mother, conspiratorially, 'It would be so much easier if they could speak Norwegian.' She's right, of course.

Gaute has cooked a special meal for us and it is, you guessed it, reindeer stew! Cooked the traditional Norwegian way, it's combined with cranberries and mushrooms, cooked in milk and cream with lashing of mashed potato, Brussels sprouts and carrots. I have to admit it is delicious. I don't think I can share this news with our grandchildren, though. I don't think they'd understand us eating Santa's favourites.

I ask Kirstin what it is like living here when the sun doesn't set. 'We have blackout curtains on the bedroom windows, so it's really no bother.'

And when the sun doesn't rise? 'Well, that's only about six weeks of the year so it's not too bad. Mind you we have a lot more energy at this time of the year than we do in the depths of winter.'

She tells me that she laughs when she sees news reports of children being kept home from school in the US because of the snow. 'If we did that here my girls wouldn't go to school for months!'

Talking with Gaute and Kirstin gives us a real insight into life above the Arctic Circle. They are a fabulous young couple. I'm sure I couldn't survive up here for a winter, but there is always the upside. They get to see the Northern Lights regularly during the dark months.

•

We are now only a short ride from Nordkapp. The manager at our hotel is a keen motorcyclist and tells us that the ride to Nordkapp is not a good experience in bad weather. I really wish people would stop saying that!

Brian: Today's the day. We are heading to Skarsvag, the closest town to Nordkapp. If the weather is clear, we will ride to the top today. If not, we've booked a hotel for two nights, so we can ride up tomorrow.

Heading across the plains the winds are blustery but not too bad. At

Lærdal Tunnel, Norway's longest at 24.5 kilometres

Arctic Circle - 63°.33.33

least the sun's out. The countryside is very different. There are no trees, only small bushes. It looks like it's pretty windswept up here most of the time.

At lunch I get talking to a local off-duty policeman who is riding home to Honningsvag, not far from Skarsvag, for a festival weekend. He warns us about more winds to come. 'Be careful. The wind can be so strong it will blow a caravan or a motorhome over.'

Oh, great. Shirl has wandered over and heard this part of the conversation and immediately looks worried. I try to downplay my concerns but I've certainly taken on board the policeman's advice.

•

We ride on, heading north, and the wind is getting stronger. Shirl tells me she is frightened, scared we are going to get blown off the road. I tell her to hunker down and hang on. I know she's not enjoying it. Nor am I. She has every right to be concerned. This is very unpleasant and potentially dangerous. The view, however, is amazing. The water is blue with white peaks being whipped up by the wind. The wind is creating small water spouts on the surface of the Mageroysundet Strait that separates Nordkapp from the mainland. There is a rainbow, spreading striking colours across the blue sky. I think to myself how much worse this would be if it were wet.

•

Over the past couple of weeks when the weather has been bad and we've ridden into one of the long tunnels I have hoped for an improvement in the conditions on the other side. There never has been.

Today, when we hit the seven-kilometre-long undersea Nordkapp Tunnel I again hope for a change in the weather conditions.

Be careful for what you wish for.

When we ride out of the tunnel the weather has changed. It's worse! It's raining now and the wind is getting stronger and stronger. We don't ride far and there's another tunnel. Inside we pull up in an emergency stop area. It's time to put on the wet weather gear we should have put on at lunchtime, but it was sunny then.

Shirl is struggling. We all are. Even Dave admits this is the worse ride he's ever done. 'I usually don't envy you having the extra weight of a pillion passenger. Today I wish Shirl was on the back with me, helping keep the bike on the road.'

I'm not sure that Shirl sees this as a compliment.

Shirley: I'm cold. I'm wet and I'm frightened.

There's no doubt about it. I've never felt so vulnerable on the bike. I try to tuck in behind Brian but the wind is swirling around us. There's no getting away from it. I have complete faith in Brian as a rider. I wouldn't do these trips if I didn't. Today is different. I can tell he's stretched. Even Dave, who has raced bikes at different times, says this is the worst ride.

What the hell are we thinking?

When we see the Skarsvag town sign our hotel is the second building we come to, just a few metres farther on. The flags outside are at right angles to the flagpoles and getting a thorough buffeting in the wind. Across the road there are some reindeer grazing. They seem oblivious to the harsh conditions.

It's still pouring and the wind is still gale force but at least we are here. Around the back there are about 10 bikes parked. So we are not the only crazy ones.

I duck inside and I'm greeted by a man in thermal long johns. He seems as surprised to see me as I am to see him. I must look like a drowned rat and he certainly wasn't expecting a woman to turn up.

There's no one on duty at reception but our key is there.

It's amazing what a hot shower and some dry clothes can do. I feel human when we walk into the small lounge to meet Dave for a well-earned whisky.

There are three motorcyclists deep in conversation with him. When I walk in the conversation stops and Dave tells me to take a bow. They all give me a standing ovation. Dave tells them what a champion I am for doing what we are doing. Thanks fellas.

Brian: I'm forever telling Shirl not to underestimate what we are doing. Riding in the strong winds is incredibly difficult for rider and pillion, but with nowhere to shelter we just have to ride on. She's done an incredible job. Shirl downplays how important her role is, on the back of the bike.

Today was awful and there's no suggestion we'll head out to Nordkapp tonight.

Nordkapp - 71°10'21"N 25°47'04"E

•

It's June 12 and today's the day. Up here we are closer to the North Pole than we are Oslo, the Norwegian capital.

10am and we are heading out. The hotel owner has taken down the flags because he doesn't want them to shred in the wind so it's hard to say how strong the wind is this morning. It's raining here, only 12 kilometres from Nordkapp. We've been told the weather can be much better up there, or worse. And it can change in an instant.

The wind is pretty ordinary as we go up the hill towards the point. The higher we get the bleaker the weather gets – colder, windier. Shirl shouts over the wind noise that she can't get the camera out because her fingers are frozen.

At the entrance gate we are nearly blown over, waiting in line. Shirl asks the cashier if he could turn the thermostat up. He gives her a half-smile that makes me think she's not the first to crack this lame joke.

In the carpark we spot a motorhome and use it as a windbreak.

Walking to the monument that marks the northernmost point in Europe, (well, to be perfectly honest it's not the northernmost point but it is the farthest you can get to by road) the wind is incredibly strong, making even the smallest movement, small gestures like opening the visor on our helmets, difficult.

The wind whips up the 307-metre rock face from the water below – on both sides of the point. I turn around and find Shirl is lagging behind. She's struggling to walk with all her bike gear on in this wind. Dave and I get on either side and drag her along with us.

We've made it to Nordkapp - 71°10'21'N 25°47'04'E.

This is certainly an achievement to celebrate, so we lash out on some champagne, king crab, caviar and salmon in the restaurant overlooking the point.

Finland and Sweden

13 – 30 June 2015

Shirley: After the appalling weather of the past two days I am dreading riding out of Skarsvag this morning. Looking out the window it seems calmer but the flags are still down so I don't really know what the wind is like. Even if it's calm now I know how quickly things can change up here.

The looks haven't been deceiving. It is much calmer. It's cold, but there is little or no wind today. The weather doesn't deteriorate even when we ride out of the *Nordkapp Tunnel*.

•

There are no border formalities but there is a very obvious difference between Norway and Finland – the scenery. It's as if there is a line drawn between the two countries. From mountains and snow we are now riding through forests and past lakes.

There are large herds of reindeer. They graze alongside the road and occasionally make a dash across the road just as we ride by. I might have thought they were a rarity when we first saw them in Norway but here they are everywhere! This part of Finland is known as Lapland and reindeer husbandry is an important part of the local indigenous Sami culture.

Finland is lovely, but so different. I miss the mountains and the snow. I especially miss the switchbacks. The speed limit is back to 100 kph so we quickly put the kilometres behind us.

•

We cross the Arctic Circle again, this time at Rovaniemi. It couldn't be any more different than the crossing in Norway. Built around the geographic mark is Santa's Village. The only snow here is the fake kind sprinkled around the seat where the jolly fellow in the red suit chats with children.

It's very touristy. There are restaurants serving reindeer that seems very wrong here in Santa's Village. When I mention this Brian points out that Australians do eat the animals that are part of our national emblem – the kangaroo and the emu. Some might, Brian, but I don't.

You can buy T-shirts, jewellery, Christmas decorations and post them home from Santa's post office. This is the perfect opportunity to lighten the load on the bike, so all the bits and pieces we've bought over the past month are jammed into a box and despatched to the southern hemisphere.

•

Tomorrow we plan to head into Sweden. The boys are bored with lakes and pine trees already.

Brian: It's raining and it's cold again. This isn't a good way to start the day. Dave suggests we spend the day here but I think we should push on. We aren't planning a long ride. The rain eases while we load the bikes. I'm sure that's a good sign.

Unfortunately, I'm wrong. As we ride out of the town the rain comes down again. It gets harder and the air gets colder. The only thing colder than the air is the atmosphere on the back of the bike. I detect unhappiness coming from the pillion in a million.

We've been riding for a little over an hour and there is no sign of the rain easing up. Shirl suggests we find somewhere dry to pull over when we get to Tornio. She doesn't complain often but she's not happy today.

'I was cold before we started and now I'm freezing. My feet are cold, my gloves are wringing wet and I'm over it. I vote for finding a hotel and calling it quits for today,' she complains inside her helmet.

She's right and Dave agrees, so we head into town and find a warm, dry hotel. Dave resists what must be a temptation to point out that he did suggest taking the day off the bike because of the weather.

We're still in Finland and Sweden is just over the river. It will still be there tomorrow.

•

We cross the border into Sweden, another border in name only, and head to Boden to get fuel and some local currency. After lunch at a small burger restaurant we're just about to get back on the bikes when

Arctic Circle at Rovaniemi, Finland

Lost on the road to Wild B&B, Sweden

On the road to Vilhelmenia, Sweden

Reindeer wander across the road, Sweden

a young woman comes up to find out where we are from and where we are going. We're used to this interest in us, but this is different.

Eleonor Norgren is a producer with Sweden's national broadcaster. She's been in the area covering the birth of the royal baby and a royal wedding. Not one to miss an opportunity she'd like to interview us for one of her programs. There's no mucking around. In a couple of minutes, she's back with a recorder and we do an interview in the supermarket carpark. Ah, celebrity status in Sweden – it's not to be sneezed at!

•

Tonight we're staying at the Wild B&B and Husky Farm at Stroberg. Dave and Shirl saw it on Booking.com and thought it would be a unique experience and a peaceful location for an overnighter. They advertise they have a BBQ so we stop in town and get supplies for a slap-up dinner.

It's obviously an out-of-the-way place. It doesn't take long before the road turns to dirt and then narrows before petering out altogether at the driveway to a very cute cottage. There's an elderly couple doing some gardening and they are surprised when we turn up. They are not sure where we are going but state the obvious – this can't be the way to wherever it is.

They get their maps and spread them out on the grass. We pore over them and finally work out where we need to go and it isn't the way the GPS has been sending us.

Shirley: Brian and Dave head back to the main road, ignore the GPS directions and take the road suggested by our gardening friends. Their directions are perfect. A very good dirt road leads us to the Wild B&B.

And wild it is - just a few cabins in the garden next to kennels that are home to 70 huskies. The B&B is a summer sideline for the main business – dog sled tours in winter.

We cook up a storm in the garden and eat in the cosy breakfast room. The tranquillity is disturbed only by the occasional howl from the dogs. It only takes one to start the whole pack going. I wonder if they calm down when it's time to sleep, but, then, how will they know when it's time to sleep. The sun still isn't setting.

It's 4am and it's as bright as midday outside. The haunting howl starts up. This is hilarious. Unbeknownst to us, Dave is on the phone to a girlfriend at home in Florida, telling her about the dogs. As if on cue they put on a performance that can be heard right across the world.

It will be midsummer soon and we're heading to Borlange to celebrate. I've read this is the place to be for the festivities and I reckon Dave is looking forward to the chance to meet some Nordic beauties over long lunches.

Brian: We've got a couple of days on the road to get to Borlange and the back tyre is getting pretty low on tread. I'm keen to nurse it through to Helsinki where we can fit the more robust Heidenau tyres. I reckon a set of Heidenaus will get me all the way through Russia and Central Asia without having to get new tyres on the road. Everything I've read says that it can be hard to get good tyres in that part of the world.

The back roads in Sweden are fantastic but they are dirt. Every time the road deteriorates I wait for the tell-tale sign of a puncture. So far, so good.

Today is one of the most enjoyable days we've had on the road for a while. The sun is shining. The sky is blue with some light clouds. There's no wind. The reflections on the lakes we pass are just brilliant. We see plenty of reindeer and even a couple of moose wander past us. They are big buggers. You wouldn't want to hit one of them.

We end up spending the night at a camp ground in Vilhelmina, right on a lake. The two-bedroom cabin is perfect for the three of us. The view over the lake is spectacular. A couple of drinks, a good home-cooked meal – it just doesn't get much better than this.

In the town of Östersund we find the Aussie Bar. Alas, it is Aussie in name only. No Australian beer. No Australian music. Just a couple of cricket bats on the wall and some posters for Fosters – the one beer Australians don't actually drink!

For dinner we go to the English pub, the Bishop's Arms. They've got

Reflections of Sweden

Church boat racing, Lake Siljan, Sweden

Froson Kirke, Sweden

Summer Palace, Stockholm

it right. Snugs, books lining the walls and good food. We make plans for tomorrow and Borlange. The first thing we must do is find out where the feasting will be happening.

Shirley: Before we head to Borlange I make the boys ride to Froson, known as the pearl in the Great Lake of Sweden. There's a 12th Century church on its shores that is the most popular place for weddings in all of Sweden. I don't think Brian and Dave are that interested in a wedding venue, but they humour me. The whitewashed church and its freestanding belltower are very cute. The view across the lake is breathtaking. I can understand why it is so popular with Swedish brides.

But the best is inside the church. The guide is filling in time playing classical guitar. We sit on the wooden pews and listen – it is like the music of angels. Brian and Dave agree - the road can wait for a while.

•

We get to Borlange. The weather is a bit iffy but that doesn't deter us. It's midsummer weekend and we need to get to the celebrations. The girl at reception tells us the place to be is Gammelgarden. We dump the bags, get back on the bikes and head out.

Well, what we see is far from what we expected. We've had visions of long trestle tables packed with pickled herring, meatballs, crispbread, smoked salmon, beetroot and apple salad, washed down with Absolut Vodka or local beer.

What we find is locals dressed in traditional clothing, with flowers in their hair. The men are in knee breeches and the women are wearing bright-coloured skirts and shawls. There is folk dancing around maypoles and family groups singing children's songs, complete with actions. We get a few laughs watching the uncoordinated fathers getting down and pretending to be rabbits and other animals with their kids or play acting doing washing and hanging out the clothes.

Wandering around the historic buildings of Gammelgarden we meet two American women with a young man and older woman in traditional dress. The older women are distant relatives. Their great-grandfathers were brothers. One stayed in Sweden. The other went to America. The families reconnected in the 1950s and the Americans have come to spend midsummer with their Swedish relatives. The

Swedish couple are mother and son. She is wearing the costume she wore on her wedding day. It was her mother's. Her son is wearing her husband's wedding outfit. It's a great midsummer story.

Ah, but there is no feasting under the midnight sun.

•

It's a long weekend and the only restaurant open in town tonight is the Indian. Dave doesn't eat onions or garlic so ordering for him is a challenge. He's not keen but I tempt him with pappadam, naan, chicken tandoori and rice. He's a convert to Indian food but is lost with the after-dinner conversation. When the waiter finds out Brian is Australian he immediately launches into a lengthy conversation about cricket and the state of the game in his homeland – Bangladesh.

Poor Dave has absolutely no idea of what they are talking about. Americans find it hard to understand a game that can go for five days without a result.

Brian: So midsummer hasn't been what we expected but today the sun is shining and there are historic boats being raced on nearby Lake Siljan. Church boats have been used in this area for hundreds of years. They date back to a time when attending church was compulsory and there were very few roads. People would row to church on a Sunday.

Since the 1930s the boats are raced on midsummer weekend. Local teams match their strength at the oars over a course laid out in the lake. Each boat takes 20 rowers and a very vocal sweep. Lazing about in the sun on the grass behind the lake we can hear the yelling and screaming of the sweeps, encouraging their teams.

Dave gets talking to a local woman whose son is rowing. She explains that it is getting harder and harder to convince the young people to get involved. She's here because her son has a hangover and can't drive but he still gets into a church boat and rows.

At least *he* found the midsummer party last night.

•

Heading back to town Dave is leading. Suddenly he chucks a U-turn and pulls up outside a 1950s retro café. We step back in time into a US diner, complete with juke box, bright-coloured laminex tables and vinyl-covered chairs. We go for the special of the day – milkshakes and waffles.

Saying goodbye to Dave, Stockholm, Sweden

Old Town, Stockholm

Turku, Finland

Uspenski Cathedral, Helsinki, Finland

Helsinki Cathedral, Finland

The owners are Brits, Andy and Helen. They love the 1950s and are dressed for the part. He has a rocker's haircut and Helen is a good-looking bobby soxer. They are living their dream but it's a tough existence. Helen still lives in England, working to fund Andy's vision. She's here for a midsummer break.

•

There's one last thing to see before we leave Borlange – the *Falu Gruva*, the heritage-listed Falun copper mine. No one is sure when mining started here but it goes back to at least the 700s. To make it easier to remove the gold, silver and copper the miners would light fires to heat the ore, making it easier to remove. It must have been a nightmare working underground at 40°C.

Our time with Dave is coming to an end. We're going to miss him. For our last couple of days together we're going to Stockholm.

Shirley: I've found us some terrific accommodation in the past couple of weeks. The cabin by the lake, the B&B with the huskies. Our room in Stockholm is not my finest moment. The hotel is right on the highway and the room is the tiniest room, with the smallest bed we've ever had. One wall is covered by a curtain which I presume is hiding the view of the traffic. No. It's hiding a concrete wall. We don't actually have a window.

•

It's such a lovely day. Summer has finally arrived for us and it's glorious, the perfect day for a visit to the Summer Palace, the private residence of the Swedish royal family. I'm in my element exploring this amazing building on a self-guided tour. Unlike so many historic buildings there are no problems taking photos inside the palace and we don't have to pay for the privilege.

Dave is knocked out by the sumptuous decorations and extravagant furniture. I'm glad. I often wonder if he's enjoying his time when I get into one of my tourist moods.

•

The only restaurants near the hotel are at the local shopping mall. None of us can be bothered riding into the city or getting the bus so we walk up to the mall, expecting to find greasy fast food outlets. We are more than pleasantly surprised. The grill restaurant has a special of lamb cutlets with rice and salad. The bar serves a very fine glass of white wine. It's one of the best meals we've had for ages and it's being served in the shopping centre food hall!

As a bonus there is a government-run liquor store nearby so we get a bottle to share back at the hotel.

•

Rather than getting the bus we ride into the centre of Stockholm. We make a couple of wrong turns and take a spin down the 'bus only' lane before hitting the city. It's only 10 o'clock but there are already plenty of tourist buses near the old city. To avoid them we ride a little farther and end up coming down a very slippery cobblestoned street. There are no other vehicles. We've found our way onto a pedestrian walkway. We brazen it out and no one seems to care.

We're on a roll. We get to a square on the edge of the old city. It's clearly not a parking area but we put the bikes in a corner near a bicycle park. Just as we're locking them up a police car drives in. Well, that's that. No it isn't. They don't give us a second look.

•

I love seeing cities from the water and Stockholm is no exception. The first thing we do is a boat trip. We go past a small red castle flying the Swedish flag. We're told the flag only flies when Sweden is at peace. It has been flying, uninterrupted, for more than 200 years. That's a record to be proud of.

Back on shore we hear bands. The soldiers are marching to the Royal Palace for the changing of the guards. It's all about timing!

Walking through the old town we see an elderly woman struggling along the cobblestoned street with her walker. The uneven path is making it very slow going and she looks exhausted. I ask if we can help. She's trying to find the Mats Jonasson crystal shop. A local trader I ask isn't sure but suggests the street at the top of the hill. The boys take an arm each and I take the walker. Along the way she tells us she started collecting this crystal when her husband was alive. He's gone now but she wants to add to the collection and buy a gift for friends celebrating their ruby wedding anniversary. When we get to the top of the hill the shop she's after is right there. We deposit her at the door, all glad that we were able to help her find the store. I can't help but take a look at the crystal. Some of the smaller pieces are just exquisite – animals carved into the crystal. I'm tempted, but one look from Brian tells me it's not a good idea. He's right. Where the hell would I put it?

•

Tonight is our last night together. Tomorrow Dave will get the ferry to Estonia and we will head south and then cross back into Finland on our way to Russia.

It's been terrific travelling with Dave. He's easy to get along with. His wicked sense of humour has lightened many a dull moment. The ease with which he can chat to total strangers has been a marvel to behold.

Just to prove a point, Dave gives a woman staying in the hotel a spin around the car park before he loads up his bike. She'll never forget the charming American and nor will we.

Brian: I'm not sure who cries the most when we say our last goodbyes – Shirl or Dave. There are long embraces and we stand in the drizzling rain and wave him off on the next part of his journey.

We've been with people since May 8, the day we left Berlin. One of the joys of trips like ours are the people we meet along the way and the old friends we meet again. In the past weeks we've had so much fun travelling with Dave and being with Bernd and Heidi, Jens and Kati and André and Tonya in Germany. Spending time with people we know and love is always a joy. And this year we made new friends in Connie and Jørgen in Denmark. The downer is when it's time to say goodbye. I know Shirl finds this particularly hard.

I enjoy being with others, but for me it's even more special to be travelling with just my old girl again. And I don't mean the bike. It is fabulous to share the adventure with my wife. The closeness is something we cherish on the road. We meet many travellers who would love to share their journey with the partner who, for many reasons, is unable to ride with them.

•

I know Shirl is a big fan of Scandinavian crime writers and she's mentioned more than once that she'd like to visit the town of her favourite fictional Swedish detective, Kurt Wallander – Ystad. It's more than 600 kilometres from Stockholm and even she agrees it's a long way to go to see a town inhabited by a fictional character, even though we did visit Port Isaac in England – the home of TV's grumpiest doctor, Doc Martin.

Rather than a long ride in Scandinavia's constantly changing weather we head to Oskarshamn – a small town on the coast. Normally it's Shirl's job to find the accommodation but I want to surprise her with something special for our last days in Sweden. I've found a great hotel, right on the water's edge. It's the perfect place for a holiday within a holiday – a few days to chill out.

It is a peaceful location. Tucked away from the main road and overlooking the bay, we spend our days taking long walks, watching the water birds and their babies. There's plenty of time to relax, enjoying a fine wine together and just take in the view.
Perfect.

•

To get to Finland for the land border crossing into Russia on July 1 we're taking the overnight ferry. At the designated loading time the ferry is making its way across the harbour. I guess we'll be late leaving. We don't count on the Finns' organisational skills. When the ferry arrives it comes into the dock sideways – a very nifty display of parking, or should I say berthing. As soon as the gangway is down a sea of people wearing red and yellow T-shirts swarm on board. They are the cleaners.

Before long we're told to mount up and head on to the ferry. There's a small area set aside for motorcycles. There are no tie downs, no straps, just a wedge of wood under the back wheel. The deckhands obviously know what they are doing and they're not expecting any rough seas on this trip.

We have a four-berth cabin to ourselves. The bathroom's bigger than some we've had in hotels and the Wi-Fi is free. It's an internal cabin with no porthole so we head to the bar and get a table right by the window. While we dine on tapas and local wines we watch the magnificent Swedish archipelago slip by. It is so peaceful as the world drifts by. On the dock the ferry didn't seem that big but the shadow we cast on some of the islands is huge. For people sitting in their gardens and enjoying the afternoon sun it's impossible to ignore the vessel as it blocks out their sun.

Chocolate infused meringues, Old Market Hall, Helsinki, Finland

Delicacies at Old Market Hall, Helsinki, Finland

The view from Hotel Korpilampi, Helsinki, Finland

Sibelius monument, Helsinki

Shirley: We arrive in Turku, Finland at breakfast time. Not much is open on this Sunday morning so we head to the traveller's staple when seeking cheap food and free Wi-Fi – Maccas. No matter where you eat this fast food in the world it tastes the same and Finland is no exception.

Turku is Finland's oldest city. We take a ride around town checking out the castle, the cathedral and the impressive art museum. The town is like a living museum taking a snooze. Unfortunately, we can't hang around. We need to get to Helsinki. As Brian always points out to me, 'We can't see everything.'

As it turns out, our hotel room isn't ready so we could have lingered longer in Turku. No point in dwelling on that. We dump the luggage off the bike and head into the historic centre of Helsinki. There is a massive street market right on the waterfront, with plenty of little spots to slip the bike into a free parking area.

The usual tourist trinkets are being sold alongside stalls selling the most amazing array of seafood. Salmon steaks are sizzling on the grill and massive pans of whitebait are frying. We can't resist a plate piled high with whitebait for only €8 (about AUD$12). Delicious.

Of course, there's a boat trip out into the bay and, of course, I convince Brian we should take it. For an hour and a half, we cruise around the bay checking out military bases, exclusive homes with their expensive yachts moored at the bottom of the garden and little beaches. But the best view is heading back into the dock. The splendid Helsinki Cathedral with its whitewashed walls and green domes stands high above the waterfront buildings, an historic landmark. Alongside is the modern Sky Wheel, a massive Ferris wheel slowly turning in the sunshine. On a hill at the other end of the bay is the 19th Century Uspenski Orthodox Cathedral. Seeing these three landmarks from the water is brilliant.

Wandering back to the bike we pop into the old Market Hall. At the wood-panelled stalls locals are selling local wines, cheeses, smoked trout and salmon that get the tastebuds salivating, or you can sit and enjoy an expensive coffee in these historic surroundings. The coffee doesn't interest us but I can't resist the chocolate-infused meringues. The size of a small football, they are as light as a feather and melt in the mouth. Isn't it true that calories eaten outside the home don't count?

Our hotel is on the edge of a lake. After our seafood feast and sugar fix at the market we go for a local tasting platter for dinner. We eat on the terrace by the lake, surrounded by forest. The only thing breaking the peace is the shrieking of locals who are taking a dip in the lake. By their reaction I'd say the water is bloody cold. With a rug over my knees to keep out the evening chill, we dine on prawns, salmon, prosciutto and goat cheese. Wonderful.

Brian: The bike's tyres have only just made it here. Every day we rode on the dirt and gravel roads I was waiting for a puncture. Even the highways of Norway are tough on tyres because of the rough surface needed for the winter months. I think it's more good luck than good management that we've made it to Helsinki without incident.

I've arranged to meet the local Heidenau dealer to fit the more aggressive Scouts front and rear. They are high profile and rugged and should get us all the way through Russia and Central Asia. They are not good in the wet, a bit slippery, but I don't think that's going to be a problem from now.

On the way we drop into the local BMW dealer to see if they have an oil filter I need. Not only do they have the part, the manager is a local woman who is able to tell Shirl where she can get her hair cut. I suggest just shaving her hair like mine, but she doesn't agree.

•

I'm expecting the GPS co-ordinates for the tyre dealer to take us to a shop or warehouse. Instead, it takes us off the main road and down a narrow road that turns to dirt. We pass a farmhouse and fields, not motorcycle shops.

Shirl is getting panicky and is convinced something is very wrong. I'm putting on a brave face, but it does seem a bit odd.

When the GPS says we are at our destination there is a ramshackle farmhouse and a large shed. I ride around the back and a man comes out. For the first time in Scandinavia, we find someone man who doesn't speak English but he does understand sign language and directs us to the back of the shed. It's all locked up, but we are early.

Right at the agreed time a van comes down the road. It's emblazoned with the Heidenau logo. The dealer explains that he is the wholesaler and doesn't have anywhere to fit or balance the tyres at his office. This is his old workshop from days when he was the mechanic for motorcycle racing teams. He's methodical and thorough. He might not have the latest wheel balancing equipment but he uses the tried and true method of suspending the tyre on a piece of wood to get the same job done.

The dealer used to race bikes and his shed is chock full of Ducatis, Bultacos and some more modern Japanese race bikes. Shirl just sighs and disappears out into the sun while I explore.

•

We're about 200 kilometres from the Russian border and then another 100 kilometres to St Petersburg.

These past three months have been fantastic. We've seen some amazing things. Ridden some fantastic roads, but really, it hasn't been that challenging.

I think all that will change.

Tomorrow we cross into Russia. Let the adventure continue.

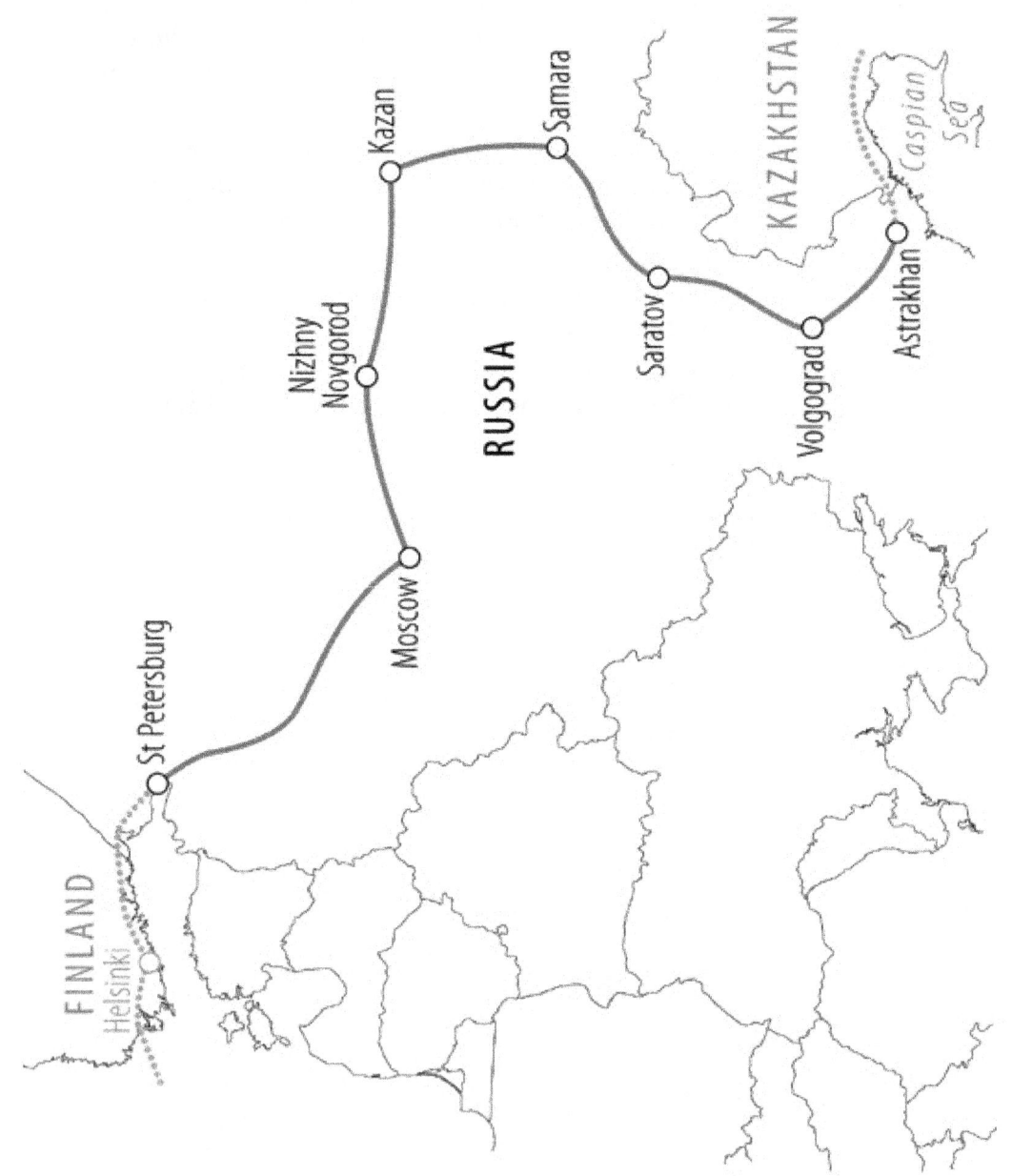

Western Russia St Petersburg to Volgograd

1 – 18 July 2015

Shirley: I'm excited and nervous about crossing into Russia. I came here as a child with my parents. My Dad was controversial communist author Frank Hardy. He was working in the Soviet Union, as it was then, in 1962 and my Mum Ross, my brother Alan and I visited him there. I went back in 1976 while it was still the Soviet Union. I know it will be different now, but the paperwork we had to complete to get our visas for Russia is reminiscent of the paperwork from the old days of the communists.

It's surprising how much I can remember from my first visit when I was only seven years old. I know a few random words and can still count to 10, order cold milk and introduce my brother, Alan, in Russian. I wonder how useful this is going to be when we are on the road. Certainly being able to introduce Alan won't be much help as he won't be with us.

Before we left home Alan told me Mum and Dad used to joke about going to the *Pectopah* for dinner. The Russian word for restaurant looks like *Pectopah* in the Cyrillic alphabet, but is pronounced restaurant. That story has already come in handy in Bulgaria where they use the Cyrillic alphabet. Plenty of restaurants don't look like restaurants from the outside. The sign is the only giveaway.

•

We have about 150 kilometres to ride from Helsinki to the border. There is hardly anyone on the Finnish side. As the guard stamps our passports he tells us there isn't the usual amount of traffic these days because of the economic situation in Russia. It's not good. International sanctions because of Russia's annexation of the Crimea and the crisis in the Ukraine are taking their toll. Life must be hard for the Russians.

•

There's about a kilometre of no man's land before we get to the Russian border. The boom gate is down. There's a guard in the security box but he's not coming out. Maybe it's lunchtime. There's a queue of cars, all with Finnish registration plates, waiting in line. A couple of Russian cars drive on by and are let straight through.

I wander along the line of cars and ask the people who have their windows open or are standing next to their cars if they speak English, but I can't find anyone who can help with some local knowledge. While we ponder the delay it starts to rain. Everyone hunkers down in their cars and we stand by the bike, getting wet. Finally, the man in the car in front of us, who had ignored me earlier, gets out of his car and tells us the crossing takes time because of the paperwork that has to be filled in for your vehicle. We don't have the paperwork filled in but we've checked out the form online and know what we need to do.

Brian: Standing in the light rain is annoying but we learnt a long time ago that you never get angry with border guards. It doesn't do you any good at all. As Shirl says, 'Always smile at the man with the stamp to get you into the country and the man with the AK47.'

The boom gate finally comes up and we realise it wasn't shut for lunch. It was shut to prevent a traffic jam at the gates. We're directed to the front of a line, shown where to put the bike over to one side. I have the passports and the motorcycle's paperwork and head to the first window.

The young guard, cooped up inside the small office, peers out at me through the tiny window. He speaks a little English which is a great relief. Shirl's small number of Russian words won't be needed here!

The guard gives us the registration papers we need to fill in and even provides a couple of pens. We think this is simple, but we don't fill in both pages. Rather than getting grumpy, the guard just points out our error and waits patiently while we finish the job.

Next stop is customs – another small window in the concrete

Uprising Square, St Petersburg

Admiralty Spire, St Petersburg

Nevsky Prospekt, St Petersburg

Anichkov Bridge, St Petersburg

Maccas, St Petersburg

border building. The guard, again an incredibly young-looking man, pushes the form we need to fill in for the motorcycle, our luggage and any foreign currency we are carrying. It's in Russian. I've seen this one online and have done a Google translate of the headings. I'm pretty confident I can fill it in.

Shirl starts to stress, but not for long. Before I can get out our translation the guard taps on the window and beckons us back. He presents me with the form in English and apologies for his error. As soon as he opens his window Russian drivers try to push past us. The guard isn't having any of it. While I fill in the form he slams his little window shut. The pushy Russians won't be shoving us out of the way while he's in charge of us!

The form is complicated – even in English. We have to list how many bags we are bringing into the country and how much cash. Do we count the bags on top of the panniers as separate bags? We take a punt and don't bother. I move back to the window and our guard slides open the window and checks out the form.

He runs his pen through the areas we didn't need to fill in, like the currency declaration. I get a clean form and move to the side to fill it in, correctly this time. He slides the window shut again, much to the annoyance of a local who tries to slip in and get his paperwork stamped.

This time I get it right and get a huge grin from the guard when he checks it out. The next form he hands over is in Russian and I've never seen one like it before. The guard leans forward and tells me what do to.

'Number goes in here,' he says, pointing to the first line. 'Then your name and passport number goes here. And here you write – I am temporarily importing my motorcycle into Russia. It is for my own use and is still registered in Australia.'

This form completed, he shuts the window again. I can see him typing all of the information into the computer. His two-finger typing is slow. I can see why they allow only so many cars in at a time.

When the window slides open again a hand appears with a massive amount of paperwork. He has one more word to say – welcome. *Spasibo*, Shirl says in her best Russian. Thank you! Her effort is greeted with another huge grin.

Next stop is the quarantine area. A very attractive, petite blonde female official checks out the paperwork, stamps one page and points to one of the top bags. 'Open'. When she sees it's just got our spare gloves she loses interest.

She gives us the tick and we are in. Simple really and it has taken only two hours. I hope this is a sign of things to come.

•

Like all motorcyclists should, I think it's a good idea to 'own' your part of the road. That means riding where the driver of the car would be, close to the middle of the road. In Russia, that is fraught with danger. While I'm sitting at or near the speed limit cars are whizzing past me up to 50 kph faster, and because I'm 'owning' my space on the road, I'm being overtaken by cars so close they're almost sucking my boot off. While trying to look forward, my eyes are constantly on the mirrors looking for fast moving cars, usually black limos with tinted windows.

Coming up behind trucks I check the mirrors and pull out to pass, but with some lunatics easily doing double the speed limit it's almost Russian roulette. I don't want to gamble with travelling at their pace. Foreigners on motorcycles are easy prey for police, with a traffic stop becoming a potential wallet-lightening exercise.

I pull into the first service station. I just need to think about how to handle riding and mixing with the traffic here without killing us. I figure that if I see the fast ones coming up behind us I need to anticipate their passing and, at the right time, move towards the edge of the road. Here's where a pillion comes in handy.

Righto Shirl, your job is to watch in the mirrors for fast-moving cars and let me know. Two sets of eyes are better than one.

Back on the road and working as a team we do okay and get used to dodging pot holes, tractors, trucks, donkeys and fast-moving limos.

Shirley: Before we left home, Brian's friend Kevin, who has spent a lot of time working in Russia, presented us with a 500 rouble note. With this in hand I don't need a bank immediately but I want to find one sooner rather than later. According to the map, the road to St Petersburg is a toll road and I have no idea how much they are likely to be.

I check out the shop at the service station but there's no automatic

Church of the Saviour on Spilled Blood, St Petersburg

Warning: this side of the street is dangerous during shelling, St Petersburg

The Hermitage Library, St Petersburg

The Hermitage, St Petersburg

bank here either. When I come out Brian's attracted the attention of a local. He's a big bear of a man, dressed in a two-piece polyester leisure suit. A 'man bag' is casually slung over his shoulder. This ensemble is set off with too many gold chains around his neck and wrists to count.

He speaks a little English and tells us he is a doctor for animals. He asks about our trip and tells us about countries he has visited outside of Russia. When I tell him we are trying to find a bank he puts his hand into his pocket and produces a wad of notes and offers us money to buy food and petrol. It's an incredible gesture of kindness and friendship to two total strangers. We thank him and explain we have enough money.

With a wave he wanders over to his car, a black Mercedes with tinted windows. I can just make out his wife sitting in the front seat.

This chance meeting augers well for our ride through this massive country.

•

The closer we get to St Petersburg the better the road becomes. The toll road is as good a piece of road as any we've ridden so far. The toll is only 50 roubles so we have plenty of cash.

While the road is good, the traffic becomes more chaotic when we hit the centre of the city. It's bedlam. Brian is doing a great job but even with his skill, we nearly sideswipe a small van and then come close to rear-ending a small car when it stops suddenly in front of us. My pulse is racing by the time we finally get to our hotel. It's a relief to get off the bike.

•

Our room is on the 8th floor and has the most impressive views of golden domes and church spires of the cathedrals and churches of this majestic city.

Our first meal is a traditional Russian chicken cutlet made from minced chicken and covered in chunky breadcrumbs served with grilled vegetables. Pretty damn good.

Brian: Our hotel is just a couple of blocks from the main street of St Petersburg – Nevsky Prospekt. One thing we always do when we get to a new city is the 'Hop On Hop Off' bus. It gives us the perfect overview of the city and the chance to get our bearings.

On every corner along Nevsky Prospekt there are people who seem to be selling some kind of tour but we can't work out where the tours go or if even they are actually tours. Finally, we spy the red bus and hop on.

As well as seeing the main sights of the city we get a history lesson. We both know about the siege of Leningrad during World War II, that the Russians refer to as the Great Patriotic War. (In the days of communism St Petersburg's name was changed to honour Vladimir Lenin, the founder of the Russian Communist Party. With the fall of communism, the name reverted.)

Beginning in 1941, for 900 days the Nazis blockaded the city. More than one million people died. Today there is still a sign on Nevsky Prospekt warning residents that this side of the street is more dangerous during the shelling. It's hard to imagine what life was like.

We drive past the world-famous Hermitage museum, the former palace of the tsars and the New Hermitage, built by the Empress Catherine the Great, with its portico supported by massive statues of Atlas. Every corner we turn we see another amazing piece of architecture, palaces, churches, parks, statues and bridges crossing the city's network of canals. St Petersburg is built on the delta of the Neva River and there are 800 bridges crossing its tributaries and canals.

We hop off the bus to visit the Church of our Saviour on Spilled Blood, with its multi-coloured onion domes, one of St Petersburg's iconic landmarks.

For years Shirley has been telling me how amazing it is that the communists didn't destroy the beautiful churches and palaces during the revolution. Well, she had that partly right. While they didn't destroy the splendid Church of our Saviour on Spilled Blood it did become known as the 'Saviour of the Potatoes' because it was used as a storage shed during those communist years!

The church gets its most unusual name from the assassination of Alexander II in the 1880s. An anarchist attempted to blow up the tsar but failed. When the tsar got out of his carriage to tick off the bomber, another anarchist took the opportunity to throw another bomb. This one killed the initial bomber and mortally wounded the tsar.

The church's onion domes glisten in the sunshine. The view is splendid from the front street and even more delightful from the side with one of the canals flowing alongside.

Tomb of the Unknown Soldier, Moscow

St Basil's Cathedral, Moscow   Political look-a-likes, Red Square, Moscow

GUM, Moscow

Inside there is an altar on the spot where Alexander II was wounded, with the original cobblestones exposed. The rest of the interior is a virtual museum of mosaics. When you first look at the religious works of art that adorn the walls, columns and dome you'd think they're paintings but they're actually mosaics – the most incredible mosaics.

Shirley: Before we go much farther I need a haircut. Tonya acted as interpreter when I got a trim in Frankfurt. Now I am on my own and not sure how easy it will be to find a hairdresser in St Petersburg who speaks enough English to understand my requirements. With the help of the girls at the hotel I find a hairdresser in a shopping centre who understands sufficient English, combined with my phrasebook Russian, to make an appointment.

The hairdresser who gets the job of cutting my hair speaks a little English but doesn't quite understand what I mean, even with a photo of how my hair should look when it's not so long. Problem solved when the girl gets out her mobile phone and rings her English teacher. Between the three of us I walk out with a pretty good haircut and the hairdresser has learned a few new words – scruffy, messy, thinner – all related to my haircut.

•

Yesterday on our bus ride we saw massive queues outside the Hermitage, the tsar's winter palace, and now one of the best art galleries in the world. The queues snaked their way across the huge square outside the main entrance.

Brian's not keen on queuing so he drags me out of bed early to get there before the crowds. His plan seems to have worked as there's only a handful of visitors ahead of us waiting for the doors to open, but not quite. Those who booked their tickets online wander past us and inside while we wait in the heat for more than an hour to get to the box office. Tickets in hand we finally enter a seething mass of humanity, all forcing their way into the galleries.

I came here back in 1962 with my family. In Moscow we'd met, Yuri, a tenor with the Novosibirsk Light Opera Company, and he gave us a guided tour of the Hermitage. I remember wearing cloth booties over our shoes and skating across the polished wood floors in the old tsars' rooms.

Today there are no protective shoe coverings and no space to run and skate. The security guards don't look as though they'd see the funny side of it even if I could get a run up!

The main building of the Hermitage is the Winter Palace of the Tsars; who locals call the 'last emperors'. The revolutionaries didn't destroy the palace and it even survived the horrendous siege of Leningrad. Some of the rooms are brilliant in colour and the opulence overwhelming. There are massive chandeliers with crystal by the kilogram, malachite vases two metres tall and crystal candle sticks that tower over me.

The *pièce de résistance* is the Peacock Clock. It's huge – probably a metre and a half tall and the same wide. Inside its glass case, the peacock is stationary but there is a video of it in action and what an amazing timepiece it is. The peacock's head moves and its fantail opens and closes as time passes. Tiny, golden animals around the peacock's claws move about. It is bloody amazing. It's housed in a conservatory with 10 huge chandeliers and marble floors that incorporate an ancient Roman mosaic, all overlooking a lovely garden.

In contrast to this opulence is the throne room. The throne sits at the end of a gallery of marble columns bedecked in royal red and gold – quite simple by comparison to the Peacock Room and Malachite Hall.

My favourite room is the library. There are staircases for the family to peruse the books on the floor-to-ceiling shelves. No balancing on ladders for this royal family.

The tsars certainly knew how to live. No wonder the peasants revolted.

•

With such an extensive network of waterways linking St Petersburg we have to take a canal boat trip. We travel along the canals to the Neva River, past the gold spires of the Fortress of St Peter and St Paul and look back at the domes and spires of the city's main cathedral, the Hermitage and the colonnades of the Stock Exchange. St Petersburg is a beautiful city.

Brian: Back on dry land we head to the State Memorial Museum of the Leningrad Defence and Siege (boy, that's a mouthful) to learn more about the siege during the Great Patriotic War.

The old ladies looking after the museum don't speak English but through a bit of sign language we work out we need two tickets but only one audio tour. We don't have the right money to leave as a deposit on the audio equipment but we obviously have honest faces. They just take the 100 rouble note and go to great lengths to show us that they have put it in a paperclip with the number of the audio handset they give us, along with a sheet of cardboard.

Portraits of the leaders of the Russian army look down on us as we walk up the rickety stairs covered with threadbare carpet. Each display has a number and when we touch the audio handset onto that number on our sheet of cardboard the entire sad tale unfolds.

For 900 days the German army was literally at the gates of the city. One million of the two-and-a-half million citizens of Leningrad died, mainly from starvation. The stories of the families who survived are harrowing. There wasn't a living creature in the city that wasn't at risk of being eaten. Even the cats that kept the mice and rats at bay in the Hermitage ended up on the dinner plates. So did the mice and rats. The photos of dead bodies, starving children, the ever-diminishing bread rations partnered with the stories of children eating cats and writing stories that predicted their own death are harrowing.

One million Russian soldiers also lost their lives defending the city.

No mention is made of how many Germans died, but they must have also suffered. And what was the end game of all this death? Well, the story goes that after capturing the city Hitler planned to eat in the dining room of the Astoria Hotel, overlooking the Hermitage, and then raze the city. He didn't think it was worth wasting ammunition on the Russians and planned to starve them out. The determination of the people of Leningrad ensured that never happened.

We are both absorbed by our own thoughts when we walk back out from the gloomy museum into the blazing sun.

On the way back to the hotel we walk past the Fabergé museum. The stark contrast of the images of starving children with the displays of jewel-encrusted eggs is thought provoking.

•

Shirl is a bit of a Beatles' tragic and has read about the city's John Lennon Street. It seems to be near our hotel so I let her take the lead and the map and try to find it. What she does find is a very dodgy laneway that seems to be a hive of drug-dealing activity. It is very sleazy and the arrival two older tourists creates a fair bit of unwanted attention. I bustle her out of there quick smart and we abandon plans of finding the laneway.

Around the corner we spot a man being marched across the road by a policeman. His hands are cuffed in front of him, half covered by a jumper. St Petersburg obviously has its underbelly.

•

We have a night of disrupted sleep but it's not a drama because we get to see the 'white night' of St Petersburg. The view from our room is splashed with a pale pink light as the sun sits on the horizon before rising again for another day of 24-hour sunlight.

Shirley: Our good friends Bernd and Heidi write to wish us well on our Russian adventure. They love this country but do pass on the fact that the ride from St Petersburg to Moscow is the worst they did in this vast country. Oh, terrific. Thanks for sharing!

•

I feel sick to the stomach about today's ride. Bernd's email spooked me. I sense that Brian is anxious too, but he'll never say anything. He knows that would make me worse. As we ride away from the hotel he asks me to keep an eye on the mirrors for the crazy drivers that come out of nowhere, travelling at what seems like the speed of sound. That request doesn't help ease my nerves!

It's a 700-kilometre ride to Moscow, a big ride for one day, so we hunker down and get going early.

Things are rarely as bad as we expect. Even though we're riding in peak hour traffic it's heavy but not manic. Just near our hotel there is a reminder of how tricky the roads are here. A plastic barrier, more than a metre long and half a metre high, has been dropped into a hole in the middle of the road as a warning of the hazard. The hole must be more than 40 centimetres deep and even wider. It doesn't bear thinking about what would have happened if we'd hit it. I leave the camera in my pocket so I'm not distracted and can keep an eye out for miscreant drivers and road hazards.

Russian roads are as varied as the landscapes they traverse. At first the road out of St Petersburg is really good – two lanes each way with

One of Stalin's Seven Sisters, Moscow

Changing of the Guard, Kremlin

Brian's new hat

Kremlin from the Moskva River, Moscow

a divider in the middle. We still have to watch for the speeding drivers every time we change lanes to overtake a slow truck. There are plenty of times where we have to abort an overtaking move because of a motorist coming out of nowhere.

Then we hit road work – huge sections where they have scored the surface getting it ready for repair. The new tyres don't like it very much. We seem to be slipping and sliding across the ridges because of the high profile on the Heidenaus.

Just to keep us on our toes there are long stretches where there are three lanes – the third is shared for 900 metres in one direction and for the next 900 metres in the other direction. It seems to work pretty well. Even the impatient drivers seem happy with this compromise.

Every town we pass through has a memorial of the Great Patriotic War. Some have tanks or jets or statues of soldiers incorporated into a monolith with lengthy lists of names. One thing they all have in common is masses of flowers laid in memory of the fallen.

One thing that does surprise me is the number of statues of Lenin in these small communities. I thought they would have all been destroyed after the fall of communism.

•

Getting petrol is a bit of a trial when you don't speak the language. We have to pay for the fuel before we get it. It doesn't take long for me to learn the word for full – *polni*. Sometimes this works, sometimes it doesn't. I use my best baby Russian to order the RON. We hope for 95, sometimes we get 95 but sometimes it's something less. Then I ask for *polni*. If they say *nyet* I charade pen and paper and right down a guestimate of the number of litres we'll take. Handing over way too much money often confuses them but it saves me trying to work out how much we owe.

If it is a modern station with a store and women working behind the counter, it's usually a simple process with lots of smiles and laughter. At older stations the women who take the money and turn on the pumps live in tiny offices with no windows and just a miniscule opening to push the money through. I can't see them. They are just a disembodied voice in the shadows. Understandably, these women are really bad tempered and my lack of language skills can really annoy them. They shout at me, as if that will help me understand Russian. I try to point out that shouting won't change the situation. It's very frustrating for me and for them.

People stop and take photos of the bike but they don't come up. The language barrier makes interaction very difficult. I really should have persevered learning a bit more Russian.

Brian: Today is stressful. It's such a long ride and the roads go from good to bad, to good again and then reasonable and then shocking. I just can't get into the rhythm of the road. I know Shirl is finding getting the fuel difficult but I like to leave it to her so I can concentrate on getting us to where we are going without a mishap.

On the outskirts of Moscow, the traffic is incredibly heavy until we are directed onto a toll road. This actually is better for us because the traffic is so much lighter. It seems Russians don't like to pay for the privilege. As it turns out, this toll road isn't actually functioning yet. The toll booths are still being built. We get to ride on perfect roads with very little traffic for free. Brilliant!

Then we get to the city and it all changes. It's peak hour so the majority of the traffic is heading out of town but the road into the centre of the city is clogged with trucks, buses and cars. There's hardly any bikes and I understand why. This traffic could be deadly.

The GPS takes us through the heart of the city – past the Red Square. Shirl is prattling on about being on Red Square when she was a little girl. She points out a stylish high-rise building with spires and gargoyles. She tells me it's one of Stalin's Seven Sisters, but I don't have the time or the concentration to find out the story.

We arrive at the back door to the hotel so I do what all good Aussie bikers do – ride across the footpath and park right outside the back door.

I am shattered. We've spent 10 hours on the road with only three stops. More than 700 kilometres in this traffic – it's been a real test and we've all come through it. Me, Shirl and Big Red.

•

Neither of us can be stuffed going out to dinner so we eat in the hotel, treating ourselves to two Russian specialities – Chicken Kiev and Beef Stroganoff, named after Count Stroganoff who lived in St Petersburg.

The waitresses speak perfect English. One tells us she spent seven years at a linguistic college and now she's waiting tables at a hotel. I

Tsar's Bell, Kremlin, Moscow.

Metro art, Moscow

hope she gets paid well because of her language skills.

Sleep comes quickly and deeply tonight.

Shirley: Getting around St Petersburg was simple. We walked everywhere.

Here in Moscow our hotel is out of town and we need to get two trains to Red Square. Normally this wouldn't be an issue, but the fact we can't read the language and the signs aren't in English means I'm a little nervous.

Getting the tickets is easy. My kiddie Russian includes *dyet-sit*, the word for 10 and the phrasebook does the rest. We get to our first stop without any problems but when we get out of the train at Lubyanka Station we take the wrong exit and end up on one of the famous steep escalators heading to street level. Now we are bamboozled.

I spot a young woman with a Metro 'be-seen-be-safe' vest on. When I ask if she speaks a little English she smiles and says, 'of course'. We're in luck. I explain where we've come from and where we are going. She beckons us through the barrier and makes a phone call. She chats to someone and then tells us to follow her.

We go back down the escalator. Now, this is a little scary. It is so steep and just keeps going down and down. These are legendary in the Moscow underground and we've managed to fluke one by accident!

We backtrack along the platform and she leads us down some stairs. That was our mistake. We turned right when we should have turned left. We go up a small escalator onto another platform. We expect our helper to bid us farewell here, but she stands with us until the train arrives, steps on and tells us to follow.

Surely she'll leave us now that we have arrived in the centre, but no. She walks with us, asking me if we are planning to go to the 'big theatre'. I'm not sure what she means. We're heading to Red Square. She checks the directions with an official along the way and takes us up another flight of stairs and here we are…right on the edge of Red Square. I can't believe it!

Now, that is service. All the time I thought it was some kind of scam, but she was just doing 'my work', as she explains. After asking us where we are from, our helper is gone, back into the network of train lines that run under this city of more than 12 million people.

Standing in the middle of Red Square brings back the memory of my brother, Alan, collapsing when we stood here with Mum all those years ago. On the stopover in India on our way to Russia to meet Dad, Mum and I ate breadsticks and drank Coke. Alan tried lots of the local foods and now had dysentery. Poor Al. He spent the next couple of weeks in an isolation hospital where the staff spoke no English and he spoke no Russian, just a little German. Our room at the hotel was fumigated and I moved in with Mum and Dad. We must have been the talk of the hotel.

Fast forward to 2015 and the first thing we see is the queue to visit Lenin's tomb. It's certainly not as long as it was in the heady days of the communist regime when locals made the pilgrimage, but it's long enough – probably about 300 metres. We'll pass today.

The unique St Basil's Cathedral sits majestically at the head of the square. The main church is being restored but we visit the rest of the building, walking through tiny corridors, exploring small alcoves. On the top floor, in a tiny stone room overlooking the rooftops of the Kremlin, a trio of tenors is performing. Their voices resonate through the archways of the church. It just adds to the atmosphere. We sit and listen, enjoying this unique experience.

At midday we head into the Alexander Gardens on the edge of the Kremlin and visit the Tomb of the Unknown Soldier. The guard is changing. The two who have had eyes everywhere, making sure the tourists are respectful, are being relieved. The soldiers slow march, high-step their way out of the Kremlin, across the gardens to the memorial. Their highly polished black, knee-length boots ring out on the stone paths. They revere their war dead here.

•

The State department store, GUM, is across the road. In the 1960s the shelves were filled with expensive items for the Soviet elite. When I was here in the 1970s it was shelf after shelf of nothing on display and women in white coats selling nothing. Today it's filled with designer stores like Cartier and Mont Blanc. There is plenty on display but no one is buying. The wealthy Muscovites can no longer afford to shop here and the tourists, like us, just come for a look.

We wander the lanes inside the complex, as they call them, that

Metro art, Moscow

radiate out from the central courtyard with its ornate fountain, all under the glass roof. The balconies on the three levels are decked with masses of brightly coloured flowers. It is wonderful, but the lack of genuine shoppers shows just how depressed the Russian economy is.

•

It's time to head back to the hotel. We are armed with the hotel's card. If we get lost all we have to do is ring them and they'll come and get us. Let's hope we don't get lost. I left our phone back in the hotel!

We find the entrance to the Metro no problem, but I'm not sure which line we need. I ask an official who says 'no English'. I just tell him we want to go to Lubyanka and that's all he needs. He points us in the right direction and we're on our way.

We go down the escalator and on to the train. One stop and we get out and find the number 7 line to our hotel. I know we have to go in the direction of the town that begins with the odd 'triple x' letter - Ж.

Easy. In three stops, we make our way to the surface but have no idea where we are. We've come out the wrong exit. Luckily, we see the onion domes of the monastery near the hotel and head towards it. We cross a road and see the entrance we used this morning. In five minutes we're back in our hotel.

•

Over a drink we do a bit of planning for the next couple of weeks. We have certain dates for our arrivals in Kazakhstan and Uzbekistan. We can't get there early and we can't get there late. Brian's been corresponding with Damien, a French biker who now lives in Canada. He's travelling towards Central Asia and they've been planning to ride some of the way together. We make rough plans to meet him at the Kazakhstan border.

Before we go to bed we have a Skype call with Adventure Rider Radio. Jim Martin talks to us about our travels so far. It seems to work well. Because of the wonderful world of the Internet anyone can download the programmes as a podcast.

Brian: Our second trip into Moscow is simple, in comparison to yesterday. We do make one blunder, taking the wrong exit, but it's not a bad blue. We emerge at the Bolshoi Theatre, just at the back of Red Square. Now we know what the young lady meant yesterday when she asked if we were going to the 'big' theatre. Bolshoi means big in Russian. It's such a recognisable building with the statue of Apollo in his chariot on the portico. The two-headed eagle, the Russian emblem, has replaced the hammer and sickle of the communist era.

Opposite the theatre is a massive statue of Karl Marx, the author of *The Communist Manifesto*. I'm surprised to see his image still having such a prominent spot so many years after the fall of communism. A guide tells us the plan was to destroy the statue but the cost to demolish the stone monolith was prohibitive so he got a reprieve.

•

The queue to visit Lenin's mausoleum is about the same length as yesterday, but today we'll wait. Lenin's embalmed body lies in state outside the Kremlin walls. We visited the Ho Chi Minh mausoleum in Hanoi, Vietnam, last year so it seems only fair that we visit Lenin.

We must be quiet and show suitable respect as we walk past Vladimir Lenin, the founder of the Russian Communist Party. He looks very pale. He's not looking as good as Uncle Ho in Hanoi, but he'd only just come back from being refurbished in Russia when we saw him. Maybe Lenin is due for a spruce up.

When we leave the mausoleum we walk past the memorials for the Russian leaders who are interred in the wall of the Kremlin. One of them is Joseph Stalin. His years as leader of Russia was a violent time and millions are said to have been killed. In 1961 the brutality of his regime was exposed. His body was removed from where it lay, next to Lenin and reinterred in a deep grave behind the mausoleum. Stalingrad, formerly Volgograd, reverted to its pre-Soviet name.

•

There are times when we both feel that Russian bureaucracy hasn't come very far from the days of the communists. The paperwork we had to complete to get our visa was a perfect example. We want to visit the Kremlin with a side tour of the armoury, which is home to many of the artefacts from the tsars.

We get into a queue in the ticket office. It's just after midday and there's a tour of the armoury at 2.30pm. After more than 20 minutes in the queue, the ticket window closes. They don't replace the sellers when it is their lunch break, they just close the window. Everyone moves over to another window. Finally, it's our turn and I ask for tickets to the armoury. No. That is not possible. We must come back. They only sell tickets for those tours 45 minutes before the tour time. That is ridiculous. We could get back into a queue and end up missing out on that tour because of the time it takes in line. We opt for tickets to the Kremlin alone. There's no time limit on these.

Shirley: I've been really looking forward to this. I remember the massive Tsar's Bell from when I was here with Mum and Dad. I remember standing inside it - that's how big it is.

The churches inside the Kremlin are just beautiful, similar in many ways to Our Saviour on the Spilled Blood and St Basil's Cathedral, only on a smaller scale. The golden onion domes of the Assumption Cathedral, the Annunciation Cathedral and the Archangel's Cathedral gleam in the sunshine. The Archangel's Cathedral is actually a necropolis and there are princes and tsars from the 1300s buried here. Inside the churches there are elaborate icons and masses of visitors. It's not that pleasant being pushed and shoved by locals trying to get close to an icon to say a prayer.

We find the massive Tsars' Cannon. It's hard to imagine how they would ever have loaded it with cannonballs. But it's the Tsar's Bell that I want to see.

We can't find it. I can't believe we haven't seen it. It must be here. And sure enough it is, hidden by the crowd. Memories come flooding back. I remember Mum and Dad and our interpreters Oksana and Vera. Alan was in hospital when we visited here. He missed out on a lot of our visit.

The six-metre-high bell is on a stone plinth, with the huge piece that broke out of the bell when it was cast resting on the ground in front of the hole it left. You certainly can't go inside now and I wonder how I got to walk inside back in 1962. Maybe it was because of who we were. Dad was pretty important in Russia in those days. We certainly got special treatment when we went to the theatre, so maybe we got special treatment in the Kremlin too. I feel very close to my parents today.

The Kremlin's Secret Garden is a quiet place to get away from the crowds. It also offers a bird's eye view of President Putin's helipad. He flies in and out of the Kremlin, which is a pretty good idea. The traffic chaos would be unbelievable with the number of cars he'd need for a motorcade.

•

Over the past few days we've been buying a few souvenirs and we need to organise to post them home. That's one drawback of motorcycle travel – the lack of space. I'm a dab hand at posting. We've sent parcels home from all over the world. We've posted everything from carpets to stickers and brochures of places we've visited. We've read that posting in Russia is a bit tricky, but surely it can't be that hard, can it?

Yes, it can. The girls at the hotel ring the post office. Their official advice is 'don't bother'. We don't speak English and it is expensive to organise a translator. The girls try Pony Express and DHL but can't get an answer. They'll keep trying to get a price for us.

•

Ever the tourists, we take a bus and boat tour around this extraordinary city. The infamous home of the KGB, the Lubyanka Prison looks pretty innocuous today with its bright yellow paint job, but it was the scene of much misery in its day. Many of the people brought here for perceived crimes against the state were tortured and executed.

What I love are Stalin's Seven Sisters – seven ornate buildings erected during the Stalin years. They were created to house the country's intelligentsia and artists. Today they are prime real estate. The façades still boast statues of the workers and the hammer and sickle emblem of the Soviet regime. We're both surprised by the number of government buildings that still bear signs of the Soviet.

And the jewels in the crown – the Kremlin and its cathedrals – look spectacular from the boat on the Moskva River.

•

Back at the hotel the girls think they've solved our parcel problem. From what we can gather a courier will come to collect our parcel tomorrow morning.

•

In the morning it seems that everyone knows about our bloody parcel. I can tell Brian is getting fed up with the amount of trouble to send home a few cheap trinkets for the grandchildren and friends. Well, damn it. I think it's worth it.

There are at least six calls to the courier company to sort out problems with the paperwork. One of the main issues are the cheap matryushka dolls we've bought for our granddaughters. These are the elaborately painted dolls inside dolls. They cost a couple of dollars but the courier company wants to check that we aren't trying to sneak national treasures out of the country. Oh, please, give me strength.

At 12.30 the box is taped up, labelled and with the paperwork done. The courier is coming to get the box and we leave the money with Anastasia on the desk. It's costing more to post the parcel than it did to buy the souvenirs. Finally, we can head out. I take the phone, just in case.

If we have to go to this much trouble to get some souvenirs out of the country what will be the drama when we try and get the motorcycle out?

Brian: I'm sick of the drama of the parcel and keen to get out for our last day in this wonderful city.

Today we are riding the Metro, deep under the city, to visit the stations that are art galleries in their own right. Many of the stations were used as bomb shelters during the Great Patriotic War and were planned to be used as nuclear shelters during the Cold War. Today they are a 'must see' on tourist agendas.

You can do tours but Shirl researches the most interesting and uses the underground map to plan out our day, jumping from station to station.

Our own station has a hammer and sickle on the wall, so that's our first stop. Next is Ploschod Revoluntsi which is filled with bronze statues of Soviet workers and athletes. There is a statue of a man with his dog that obviously doles out good luck. The dog's snout shines bright while the rest of the statues have weathered with age.

In the middle of all of this Shirl gets a call from the hotel and we expect the worse, but it's just Anastasia telling us the parcel has gone and all is well. Thank goodness for that.

At other stations there are murals of workers dressed in traditional costumes dancing in fields of crops. There are chandeliers, marble columns and paintings in gilt frames. They all depict happy people enjoying the fruits of their labours in perfect weather and idyllic surroundings. The images must have been galling for the workers over some of the more difficult years. It's been a fascinating couple of hours riding the trains and exploring the stations and all for a 50-rouble ticket. It's a lot of fun for just a couple of dollars!

•

On our ride out of town I want to get a photo of the bike with the Kremlin in the background. Over the past few days I've found a couple of spots that will be perfect. When we get there the entire area is ringed by police. President Putin has visitors, the leaders of Brazil, India and China, and there is no way we can stop the bike, get off and take a photo. Bugger!

•

We've really loved our days in St Petersburg and Moscow but now it's time to hit the road and get some kilometres behind us or we'll never make it through Siberia before the snow comes. I've done some calculations and Shirl's checked out the cities she'd really like to visit and we have a plan. We're heading south to meet up eventually with Damien Fauchot in Astrakhan for the ride through Kazakhstan and Uzbekistan.

It's a long hard ride to our first overnight stop, Nizhny Novgorod, the home of Russian writer Maxim Gorky. Like the ride to Moscow the road is either potholed, or brilliant, but never good for long enough to make it enjoyable. The cars come up behind us from nowhere. I have to be ultra-vigilant when I move out to overtake. One look in the mirrors and there's nothing and then I begin to move out and there's a huge black Mercedes right there.

I'm glad when we get to the hotel and abandon the bike. Tomorrow we'll ride to Kazan where Shirl would like to stay for a couple of days.

Shirley: We wake to the sound of rain – heavy rain. I dread these kind of days at the best of time but the roads and traffic here just make it all seem so much worse for me. Despite his bravado, I know Brian feels apprehensive.

Checking out of the hotel we're given two forms bearing official stamps. We're told we must keep these and present them when we leave Russia. Funny, we didn't get one in St Petersburg or the capital.

By the time we leave, the rain has stopped but the drainage isn't

A ring of security around Red Square

Red Square, Moscow

good so the water just lies on the road. The puddles are deceptive. It's impossible to know if they are just a shallow little puddle or one the size of a canyon that will swallow us and the bike whole. It's a stressful ride.

We haven't ridden long before the rain starts again. The traffic builds up pretty quickly and the road goes from bad to worse to OK and then good – situation normal. I have to admit today is a hard one for me. Overtaking at high speed, quickly getting past things is the right option but it is just a little scary.

We make a stop to put on our wets before we are soaked through and swap into our warmer gloves. As we ride off Brian shouts at me because I haven't closed the clips on the bags on the side of the tank when I got our pants out.

I'm really sorry and apologise profusely until I look down at the bag on top of the left pannier that he'd opened to get out his waterproof jacket. It's flapping in the breeze. I always feel better when he stuffs up too. It takes the pressure off.

I can't do up the zip while we're riding so Brian has to pull over. Luckily everything is still in the bag.

•

Heading the other way, back to Moscow is a convoy of blue vans under police escort. Prisoners perhaps? Then at least four convoys of four or five car carriers go past, also under police escort. There are sides trying to block the cars from view but we see they are all black Mercedes – some SUVs and some sedans. These are probably the vehicles used for Putin's love fest with the leaders.

•

We stop for lunch in a cafeteria at a petrol station. I've left the phrasebook on the bike so we do a lot of pointing and smiling. We get two plates of chicken and potato. It's weighed and then microwaved. That's lunch.

While we are eating a man comes up and shows us his phone. He has a message written but it is in Russian. He's deaf. I tell him we are Australiski, (another word that has stayed with me from childhood), but of course he can't hear me. He can't hear and we can't read, but we do manage a bit of communication. When we leave he joins his fists in a shake, wishing us good luck.

Another bloke takes photos of the bike and smiles at us as he walks past, we may not be able to converse but the friendship is obvious.

•

Back on the road the traffic is appalling, even worse than usual. To get through Brian splits the traffic and even takes to the dirt. There are certain advantages to being on the bike.

•

I have a huge agenda for today, exploring Kazan. It's cold and wet again but we don't let that deter us. We drag out the jumpers and rain jackets. We didn't think we'd be needing these for a while, but it's like winter today.

We wrap ourselves in the blankets provided and take our 'hop on hop off' of the city. It's a fascinating city with an horrendous past. The Tartar people were persecuted and executed by Ivan the Terrible in the 1500s. Their religion, a form of Islam, was outlawed until the reign of Catherine the great in the 1800s.

Lenin played chess here. Maxim Gorky lived here and so did Feodor Ivanovich Chaliapin. The story goes that he and Gorky tried to join the church choir. Chaliapin was told to try some other hobby. He went on to become a world-renowned opera singer!

The architecture is unique, with wooden houses from the 1800s, but best of all is the city's white-walled Kremlin. Inside is the exquisite blue and golden-domed Annunciation Cathedral, the President of Tartarstan's palace and the Qol Sharif mosque – Christian churches and mosques standing side by side, in peace.

•

My favourite story from Kazan is the tale of the Kazan cats. The story goes that the Empress Elizabeth in 1700 decreed that cats must live in the Hermitage to keep the mice and rats at bay. She heard that the Kazan cats were excellent mousers and had them taken to St Petersburg. For centuries their descendants worked keeping the Hermitage rodent free. Unfortunately, they didn't survive the 900-day siege of Leningrad during the Great Patriotic War. They, like every other living creature, ended up on someone's dinner plate!

Brian: It's time to move again and we wake to the familiar sound of rain, but for once, it peters out and the sun is shining when we leave

Kremlin, Kazan

Souvenir store, Kazan

Kazan Cat, Kazan

Motherland Calling, Volgograd

Siege of Stalingrad memorial, Volgograd
Siege of Stalingrad memorial, Volgograd

for our overnight stop in Samara. Even the road is good today and the traffic is so light. It's the first decent day we've had on the bike in Russia.

We ride past fields of corn and sunflowers. The colours are vibrant. It is impossible not to be uplifted by the wonderful scenery.

I'm enjoying the ride and don't even get angry when a dickhead in an SUV under passes us. It's a dangerous manoeuvre and when a car comes at us like that, on the side we are not expecting, it's frightening.

Nothing is going to faze me today, even a massive traffic jam. Rather than getting stressed I take to the dirt and get past the accident that is causing all the problems. It seems that drivers aren't permitted to push their cars off the road, even after a most minor accident, until the police arrive to take photos. This causes traffic chaos.

•

Since we left Moscow we've been given registration slips from the hotels. We're told we must keep these and hand them in when we leave Russia. Today there is a man sitting behind the counter when we arrive at our hotel and Shirl and I joke that if it was the old days he would be the KGB agent. Maybe it's not so funny. When we go out to cover the bike he wanders out and walks past us up to the back of the hotel carpark, does nothing and then wanders back.

Looking back on our first morning in Kazan there was a man sitting on his own in the corner of the breakfast room but he didn't eat anything. When we left the hotel any one of six or so blokes could have been the 'government man'. At the hotel in Nizhny Novgorod a man lurking outside while we loaded the bike was driving one of the black SUVs with blacked-out windows that the government seems to prefer. Paranoid? Maybe, but it's a fun game to play — spot the spy!

•

Before we arrived in Russia we read that the police have permission to shoot you if you don't stop when requested to do so. So far we've ridden past plenty of police but none has asked us to stop — until today.

We're still on the outskirts of Samara on our way to Saratov when I hear the whoop of a siren. I check the mirrors but can't see anything behind us, then I hear a voice on a loudhailer. This time I can see the police car. I pull up on a bus stop and we both get off the bike. The young policeman gets out of the car and walks to the back of the bike, checking out our numberplate. I point to the AAA plate and tell him we're Australian and don't speak Russian. He looks surprised. 'Australia?'

I hand over our registration and insurance papers, which he probably can't read. He takes his time walking around the bike, giving it the once over. We get the documents back and he waves us on with a polite nod. I get the distinct feeling he just wanted to check out the bike.

We don't get too far down the road when we see the usual police checkpoint. The police have a couple of trucks pulled over so I don't pay much attention. A big, burly copper, whose shirt buttons look on the verge of popping, points his baton at us. Shirl says she's pretty sure he wants us to pull over. I'm a fair way up the street and don't make any move to go back. The walk will do him good. He wants documents but isn't happy with my licences or passport. When I get out the papers we got at the border he seems happy. With a grunt, he sends us on our way. He's not been as friendly as the younger policeman in the car.

At least they didn't shake us down for a 'fine'.

Shirley: When we ride into Volgograd, formerly Stalingrad before his fall from grace, the sun is shining. The ride here has been pretty normal. Good spots and bad spots on the road and the usual crazy drivers who want to kill us or themselves.

Riding into town I can see the massive 'Motherland Calls' statue, brandishing her sword, in the distance. Next to it is a traditional Orthodox church. It's dwarfed by the statue so I presume it's like a miniature next to the statue. I'll be proved wrong about that.

•

The motorcycle needs some TLC and as luck would have it there's a bike shop across the road from our hotel. Before Brian takes it over to see if they can help with an oil change he decides to wash it down. It's filthy after all of the days riding through the rain and mud.

A man in a shop at the back of the hotel is happy to give us a bucket with some soapy water. He speaks pretty good English and is interested when he finds out we're Australian.

'We love Putin,' he says. 'Putin is Zeus.'

Motherland Calling, Volgograd

Hall of Military Glory, Volgograd

Hall of Military Glory, Volgograd

Big Red with the Bondi to Baltic Dodge and Whippet, Volgograd

Astrakhan beer   Stalin Café, Volgograd

Really? Surely he can't be serious. We've been told not to discuss politics with Russians so we both just nod and smile. What he says next comes as a surprise.

'Abbott – he is shit!'

He's referring to Australia's then Prime Minister, Tony Abbott, who threatened to 'shirt front' the Russian President. It obviously made the news here. Heads down – we get on with washing the bike.

•

At the Bike Post bike shop, the men don't speak English but they understand our predicament. They insist that Brian changes the oil here. They make room for our bike in their workshop, take the old oil and give us rags and paper towel to mop up any spills. The only charge is for the oil itself. The owner takes a few photos and by the time we get back to the hotel he's already posted photos of his Australian visitors on his webpage! The Russians, on the whole, are very friendly people – just a little reserved.

•

Daria, the receptionist at our hotel, recommends a restaurant for us, right near the Volga River. She books a table and a taxi for us to get there. We get out close to the river and walk past the most unusual statue of a bomb, presumably a memorial to the Great Patriotic War.

At the restaurant, the staff have their English menu ready and one of the waiters is keen to show off his language skills. The food is exceptionally good and we really enjoy the salads, something we haven't had for a while. The white wine is pleasant and cold, which is nice for a change. All in all, it's a great night. When it's time to leave the staff have a cab ready to go. Daria asked them to make sure we got back to the hotel.

It's been a terrific day today – probably the best we've had since leaving Moscow.

•

Motherland Calls is calling us. I've read that she was created in 1967 to commemorate the defeat of the Germans after the 200-day battle of Stalingrad. She stands on top of Hill 101, which is now the site of the Mamayev Kurgan, the memorial for the fallen citizens and soldiers. The area is probably best known because one of the many films about the battle.

Motherland Calls towers over everything. She is magnificent, calling to the faithful, brandishing her sword, her skirts blowing in the wind. At more than 80 metres tall she is one of the most wonderful monuments I've ever seen. We walk around the park looking up at her from all angles. She magnificent – one of the great highlights of the trip so far for me.

The Russians are obviously drawn to her and all she stands for. They lay flowers at her feet. Brides and grooms come here to have their photo taken with her.

In the hill below her is the Hall of Military Glory, commemorating the thousands who died here. The eternal flame burns inside a massive hand in the centre of the room. Around the walls are the lists of the dead, in mosaic.

Over the sombre music that is playing we hear the stamp of boots. The guard is changing. In slow motion, high kicking like their Moscow counterparts, they march up the ramp on the outer edge of the building. The sound of their boots echo throughout. This is an incredibly moving place even though we don't have a personal connection to the Great Patriotic War.

Outside, there are more statues depicting the hardship and heartbreak of the battle that took so many lives on both sides. Walking to the pool of remembrance there are more images of the battle and victory carved into the rock face. Piped into the area is a male choir, possibly the old Red Army Choir, singing of the victory over the fascists.

•

Back at the carpark we are surprised when we notice the Stalin Café. Inside the door is a huge portrait of the former leader, the first one we've seen. All the staff are wearing Great Patriotic War uniforms. It a great gimmick to make this café different.

I buy a miniature Motherland Calling. She will live in the bottom of my pannier until we get home.

•

Back at the hotel the receptionist tells me she has organised for us to have dinner with the other Australians. The other Australians?

As if by magic, one of them appears on the stairs. John McCombe is part of the group of friends who are helping Ian Neuss and Bill Amann drive their vintage cars from 'Bondi to the Baltic'. Ian is driving a 1920

Bike Post, Volgograd

Dinner with the Bondi to Baltic team, Volgograd

Kazakhstan border

Floating bridge on the way to Kazakhstan border

Dodge and Bill a 1927 Whippet. You just can't get away from Aussies!

These amazing blokes have spent the past couple of years getting their cars through China, Central Asia and Russia.

The singer at the restaurant is a little surprised when the Australians leap to their feet and give her a standing ovation. The Bondi to Baltic team is great company and we have a terrific night swapping tales and sharing good food and wine.

Ah, I've missed the Aussie accent and the dry sense of humour.

•

We've made arrangements to meet up with Damien Fauchot tonight in Astrakhan so we say goodbye to the Australians and head off. The road is exceptionally good today. It's one of the best we've ridden and because it's Saturday there's little traffic and hardly any trucks. It's a good ride.

At Astrakhan Damien's bike, a BMW 1200 GS with its Ural sidecar, is outside our hotel, overlooking the Volga River.

The Wi-Fi only works near the lifts. We're checking our emails when the lift doors open and there he is – tall and lanky. His whole face lights up when he sees us. His grin is contagious. He speaks with that wonderful French accent that is like liquid gold. I could listen to it forever.

We've never met before but after a couple of hours strolling along the riverbank and dinner at a reasonably good café we feel very comfortable together. There's the connection of a shared love of travel and motorcycles.

I think Damien is keen to travel with someone, to share the experience. It can be a lonely existence travelling solo. His wife, Sylvie, is back in Canada and he misses her. I can't imagine Brian travelling for such a long time on his own. I can't imagine myself allowing such a thing! We're lucky that we can travel together, that we have the shared love of this lifestyle.

Tomorrow we all ride into Kazakhstan.

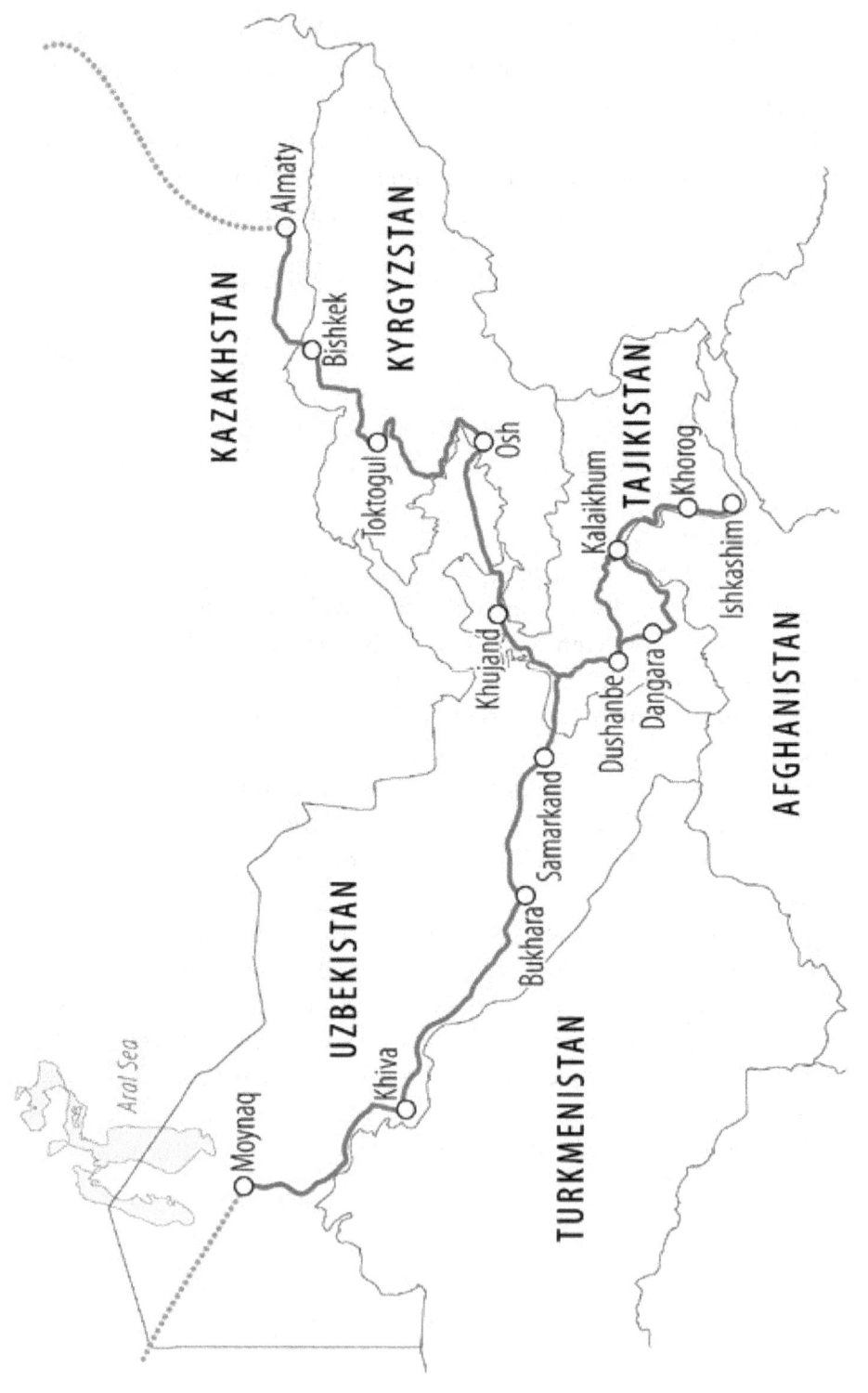

Kazakhstan

19 – 21 July 2015

Shirley: Before we leave Russia for Kazakhstan there is a photo opportunity to be had, right across the road from our hotel.

The mighty Volga River is flowing right by the door and there's a wide footpath that's a perfect place to put the bikes, with the river in the background. I think everyone who has ever learned the piano knows the Song of the Volga Boatmen – yo-o heave ho. I'm humming the ditty as I wander over the road with our camera and Damien's ready for a quick photo just in case someone decides we shouldn't be putting the bikes up here. Of course, I only know the refrain so it's a pretty boring rendition – yo-o heave ho.

No one is bothered with the bikes being on the footpath. The photo opportunity goes off without a hitch.

One last look at the river and we're on our way. It's more than 500 kilometres to our planned overnight stop at Atyrau and there's a border crossing to contend with as well.

Brian: It's an easy ride to the border on a good-quality road – a nice farewell present from Western Russia.

Leaving a country is usually a lot easier than getting into a country but we don't know what to expect now.

There's a huge line of trucks waiting to cross into Kazakhstan but everyone motions for us to move to the head of the line. An official gives us a piece of paper with the registration number of the bike written on it.

The first stop is the passport office. I hand over our passports and the document we were given when we arrived here two and a half weeks ago. Is it really such a short time? I try to give them the receipts we've been collecting at most of the hotels, but they aren't in the slightest bit interested. Oh, well, I guess they'll make a souvenir of sorts.

The female official doesn't smile – she's very serious about her job. She checks our photos to make sure we are who we say we are, stamps both the passports and the slip of paper. She then hands back the document for the motorcycle. Terrific. Hopefully we can use it again when we come back into Russia. That would make life a lot easier.

At customs there's no check of the luggage, just another stamp on our slip of paper and we're free to move across no man's land to Kazakhstan.

When we cross the border we're given an immigration form to fill out. Just inside the border there's a very modern building housing the customs and immigration offices for the foot traffic. That includes Shirl. While she's faffing about taking her helmet off, getting her passport organised a mini-bus carrying about 10 people pulls up. Hurry up, or you'll get stuck behind this mob, girl.

Shirley: There's no way I can run and get ahead of the crowd but I needn't have worried. Inside the delightfully air-conditioned room a young female official beckons me to move to the top of the queue. The locals who are ahead of me don't seem to mind a bit. There are plenty of smiles and nods of welcome. This is a nice change after the reserved Russians and its austere officials.

In the rush to get me off the bike I forgot to get my immigration form from Brian. The man processing the passport isn't fazed at all. He fills the form in for me, stamps it, stamps my passport and I'm in. Simple.

I wander out the door and find Brian talking to an official at the bike. He's more interested in checking out the bike than searching it.

The official tells us we are free to go.

I say, 'Welcome to Kazakhstan?'

He seems a little embarrassed.

'Oh yes. Welcome to Kazakhstan.' He shakes our hands and then looks at me and the bike and asks to see how I get on to the bike.

It is a bit of street theatre for me to get on. It's very tall so I put my left foot on the left foot peg and then bounce one, two three times and then allez-oop – up and over.

The official breaks into a huge grin and roars with laughter. 'Oopha!'

Brian and Damien are popular with the locals

Camels on the road to Atyrau

A local peach, Atyrau

The streets are awash, Atyrau

I reckon I've made his day.

Outside the border the money changer offers just under the official exchange rate for rouble to the local currency – the Kazak teng.

We don't have to wait long for Damien to arrive and we're on the road.

Brian: We ride out and the road is horrendous with enormous potholes all over it. It's going to be a very slow ride. The speed limit is 90 but I'm only doing about 50. This can't be good for the bike.

Kazakhstan used to be part of the Soviet Union and in those days the local infrastructure was maintained by the Soviets. That's all changed. It looks as though this once-sealed road hasn't been touched since the fall of communism in 1991. The wear and tear of more than two decades of traffic has taken its toll. The road is literally falling apart.

It's hard for us and even harder for Damien with his sidecar. At least we have only one track to find around the potholes and can miss some of them. Damien just has to grit his teeth and ride through them.

Every now and then the road improves slightly and then it's back to potholes, gigantic potholes.

There's not a lot of motorised traffic but there's plenty of other road hazards. Camels, cows, goats and horses, many with foals, grazing on what little growth there is in the desert sands. Many of them are actually on the road, drinking out of little puddles of murky water. It obviously rains here sometimes but there's no sign of clouds today.

We don't pass any towns, not even small ones, but every few kilometres there are massive cemeteries. Some of them have ornate mini-mausoleums with turrets and spires. Others are just stone blocks. It seems very odd to have such vast cemeteries and no towns in sight.

Shirley: We need a break from the bone-jarring road and pull into a fairly modern-looking service station. The locals are incredibly friendly. They all want to take photos of Brian and Damien and the bikes. They particularly love the sidecar. Many of them speak English and are delighted that we have come from so far away to visit their country.

I need a pee. The toilet is a single outdoor dunny, reminiscent of the old country toilets at home. It's not a clean drop toilet though, just a hole in the ground, which would be fine, but this one is filthy. I'll hang on!

We ride on, passing through a couple of smaller towns that don't seem to have any hotels. This could be a problem when we're looking for somewhere to spend the night.

•

We get to Atyrau and the streets are awash. There's water everywhere. This is tricky. It's impossible to tell how deep the puddles are. The water is flowing across the road from gutters that are obviously blocked. We still don't see any clouds but there's obviously been a downpour this afternoon.

Our boots get washed more than once. Brian can't really avoid the water – it's everywhere. Atyrau looks like a modern city but the drainage system doesn't seem to work too well.

•

We check into our hotel, but it's a bit too expensive for Damien. He's trying to negotiate a cheaper price when Ricardo, a motorcyclist from Spain, arrives. Even sharing a room it's out of their budget, so they head off in search of a cheaper room. We'll meet Damien in the morning.

The room is tiny and fairly ordinary. You don't get much for your money here. This room cost AUD$105.

A great piece of steak with a bottle of very good Italian red makes the bone-shaking ride fade into memory.

Brian: I can't believe it. It's just occurred to me that we didn't buy motorcycle insurance when we crossed the border. It's something we always do, but having the Green Card insurance that covered us through Europe, Scandinavia and Russia I just forgot all about it.

A quick search on the internet shows it was on sale at the border. Now we have to find it in town. We might not get pulled over and we might not have an accident but it's not worth the risk. It will cost only a few dollars to buy the compulsory third-party insurance for the few days we are in Kazakhstan.

•

Damien is as perplexed as we are. He can't work out how we forgot to ask about it at the border. He agrees we need to get the insurance before we head to Beyneu, our next overnight stop on the way to Uzbekistan.

Ricardo has left early, heading for Beyneu. We'll probably catch up with him tonight.

On the road from Atyrau to Beyneu

A cemetery on the road from Atyrau to Beyneu

Brian with a Rix tea

Trackside market, Beyneu railway station

Shirl takes charge and gets the girl at reception, who speaks remarkably good English to help us contact the insurance company I found on the internet.

Shirley: Anouchka from Centris Insurance Company speaks very good English. It's not a problem getting what we need from her. She explains the office is near the main square.

Brian and Damien have both keyed the address into the GPS. We'll be there in no time and then on the road.

Unfortunately, both GPS take us to a non-descript street that isn't anywhere near the main square. There's a service station on the corner but no one here speaks English. I suggest it will probably be easier if we go back to the hotel and ring Anouchka again.

It's like travelling with Dave all over again. Democracy at work – I lose the vote two to one. I should have expected that result. It's a well-known fact that men don't ask for directions! They are sure they can find it. A very smart looking SUV pulls into the servo and the well-dressed young man speaks perfect English. He takes charge and rings his office, gets someone there to look up the company and gets the directions. Armed with the local knowledge we hit the road.

We follow his directions but we're still not in quite the right place. We are near a square but we can't find the company. We're actually outside a shopping complex we saw yesterday on our way to the hotel. A woman comes up and asks if she can help. Her directions include going past the mosque and the square with the monument in it.

We don't find the mosque or the square with the monument. What we do find is an office complex with security guards at a boom gate. In the yard behind the fence a group of workers are taking a smoko break.

The guards don't speak English but one of the smokers asks if he can help. He speaks with the broadest Scottish brogue. This is a Scottish construction company and all the bosses are from Scotland. We go inside and he gets the receptionist to look up the company and draw us a map.

Surely we can find the place now.

No. We take a wrong turn somewhere. We pass the mosque and the square but still can't find the insurance office, only a travel agent. I ask him if he knows the building. He takes me outside and points over the rooftops. We've actually ridden past the bloody place a couple of times!

I quick dash around the corner and we see the monument and find the right building. We push the door open and there is a young woman sitting at a desk.

'Are you Anouchka?'

'Yes.'

Thank goodness. I could have fallen at her feet and wept.

Brian is in a filthy mood, but he'll get over it.

Brian: We've just wasted the morning riding around trying to find the insurance office. It has been frustrating in the extreme. I'm kicking myself I didn't remember to get the insurance at the border yesterday.

Shirl volunteers to go outside and wait with the bikes. They are both fully loaded and we don't want things to go walkabout. She might also want to get away from me for a while. It's not her fault we've been so geographically challenged, but she keeps apologising for it anyway.

Anouchka initially says the insurance will cost 1000 teng – about AUD$8.00. When she realises we only need it for a couple of days she only charges us 250 teng. I don't have any small notes and Anouchka doesn't have any change so Damien has to pay for ours.

At last, after riding around for more than two hours trying to find the insurance office, we are finally ready to get moving. It's nearly midday and we have more than 350 kilometres to get to Beyneu, our overnight stop. We should get moving.

Damien's not so sure about leaving now.

'We're not going to Beyneu now, are we?'

Shirl agrees with Damien. We have no idea what the road will be like but it is unlikely to be any better than the ribbon of potholes we encountered yesterday. To leave now we'll probably end up riding in the dark and they are predicting thunderstorms for Beyneu this afternoon.

Majority rules. We are staying another night here.

Shirley: I'm glad Brian didn't dig his toes in about leaving now. It will be good to have a break and leave bright and early tomorrow when

Trackside market, Beyneu railway station

we are all rested up. This morning has been stressful and that's not a good frame of mind for the road that probably lies ahead.

There's a beach on the riverbank in the heart of the city. It could be a good spot for lunch but the eateries are all closed. Half a dozen boys are swimming in the river and a stray dog and her pups play on the sand. Apart from that – nothing.

Damien suggests we try the hotel he stayed in last night. They do have rooms and the double is 4000 teng cheaper than the

room we had last night. It's double the size – enormous! We can spread our stuff out and still have room for dance classes!

•

We're all hungry and the café next door to the hotel looks OK. The ladies inside don't speak English and they don't have an English menu. The phrasebook and our *Picture Talk* book, with its simple illustrations of just about everything a traveller could need comes in very handy.

Beer is easy – *Pivo*. Coke is Coke. I show the waitress the picture talk food pages and she points to the chicken. That will be fine. I slap my hip and point back to the chicken. If all goes to plan, we should get a drumstick and thigh piece. Success. The chicken is just as we hoped and it's served with potatoes and salad.

•

We take a walk towards the beach and come across a street vendor selling fruit and vegetables. He has a round, flat piece of fruit that looks like an apple. I ask if it is a Kazak apple, something this country is famous for. No. It's a peach from Uzbekistan. Three cost 250 teng – the same as our insurance. It is very tasty, a little like an early season peach but dry.

•

There's an American Grill restaurant across the road from the hotel. Damien had dinner here last night with Ricardo and recommends it. The food is pretty good, not that any of us are very hungry after our slap up chicken lunch. Some share tapas style plates. With a couple of vodkas it's plenty.

We all need an early night. Tomorrow we will tackle the road to Beyneu and, hopefully catch up with Ricardo the Spaniard.

Brian: I'm glad we had a good feed yesterday. The breakfast at the hotel is pretty ordinary. Shirl is finding things like the porridge type stuff pretty unappetising. I'm concerned she's not eating enough but she assures me she's fine. She certainly hoed into lunch yesterday.

If we can get to Beyneu today, we'll only be 30 kilometres from the Uzbekistan border for the next day. Ricardo recommended a hotel to Damien, the simply named Beyneu Hotel. Shirl has read about another one, but we'll go with Damien's choice. He picked the best hotel in Atyrau.

•

After the dread of having to battle another horrendous road we are pleasantly surprised. The road is pretty good all the way. All in all, it's an uneventful day.

When we get to Beyneu we want to fuel up so we're ready to leave first thing tomorrow. The smaller stations in town look very ordinary so we head back to the highway and go to the more modern one. They only sell 92 RON fuel. Our BMWs should run on 95 at least, or even higher. Beggars can't be choosers. We'll take the 92.

The fuel tanker is there so we just have to wait. It's a long slow process. Some of the locals ask about the usual questions. Where are you from? Where are you going? How much does the bike cost? How fast does it go?

One of the men has another question which I wasn't expecting. 'How old is the woman?' he asks. When I tell him she's 60 he looks at Shirl sitting in the shade in her bike gear, nods and says just one word. 'Respect.'

I'm proud of my old girl. I'm sure she doesn't really understand how impressed people are by our journey.

Shirley: Beyneu is a dustbowl. The hotel is clean enough and cheap. It also has free Wi-Fi and there's a gate we can lock to keep the bikes safe overnight. Ricardo isn't there. He's left his spare tyres and some of his luggage and headed out into the desert. Pity. We were looking forward to talking to him.

Taking a break from the harsh roads with Damien

Camels crossing the road

The streets are deserted. There are a couple of people at the bank machine but there's no one else around. We find them all at the railway station. The train is in and there's a thriving market on the platform. The passengers are wandering through the stalls buying fresh produce and drinks for their journey. There's a fair bit of pointing and giggling behind hands as people see us looking down from the roadway onto the platform. You get used to being the subject of some interest in places like this. I guess they don't get too many foreigners wandering around.

Over dinner Damien tells us he's had an email from another biker who is on the road ahead of us. It took him four hours to get from here to the Uzbek border.

Surely that can't be right?

Uzbekistan

22 July – 1 August 2015

Brian: The farther we head south east it's getting hotter. It's in the mid-30s before lunchtime. Luckily the man at our hotel offered to freeze a couple of water bottles for us last night. It's fantastic to have cold water to quench our thirst. We have to stop a couple of times before we even get to the border. It's hot and we all need time off the bike. A snack and some cold water revives us.

Damien's mate was right. The road to the border is atrocious. It is worse than any we've travelled so far. There are massive potholes, long sections of gravel and some wide cracks in the surface. A lot of the time I take to the dirt at the side of the road which is a bit easier on us and the bike. Damien is finding it very hard. The sidecar isn't all that easy on this stuff. It takes us three hours to cover the 80 kilometres through the desert.

•

We get waved to the front of the line at the border. I expect it to be easy because we're leaving the country. It isn't. They want our passports and the temporary importation document from Russia. We get the passports back but not the Russian document. I was hoping to use it again when we cross back into Russia.

The customs officers want to search the bike. First pannier they ask me to open is Shirl's, of course. It is jam packed with clothes and bits and pieces she's collected on the way – things she wants to keep close like the Fabergé egg she bought in St Petersburg and her miniature of Motherland Calling from Volgograd. The official loses interest when he sees it is just women's clothes. He does a cursory search of one of our top bags and that's that. We're free to go.

We've been told that the process of getting into Uzbekistan could be one of the more difficult border crossings. Our first encounter indicates

Moynaq – once a fishing village on the shore of the Aral Sea, now a cemetery for ships

Moynaq – monument showing how far the Aral Sea has receded

A group of women on holiday want their photo taken with the Aussies, Moynaq

this could be the case. A guard walks up to the bike, demanding to see the video camera. He keeps shouting that we must not film in here. We have no intention of filming. Our video camera is tucked away inside the tank bag and it will certainly stay there for the time being.

It seems the guards are expecting motorcyclists to have helmet cameras. I guess Russian bikers do video every ride because of the number of motorists who drive like homicidal maniacs trying to kill them.

We are beckoned towards the immigration office ahead of the Uzbek and Kazak people waiting to cross the border. Our visas are checked and we get the all-important stamp in our passports.

The next step, customs, is the one we've been warned about.

Shirley: The advice we got from friends who have ridden through this part of the world was simple. Don't lie on your customs form.

The officials point us towards benches under a metal awning that offers us some shade and a slight respite from the heat while we fill in our forms. On the wall there are posters in Russian, Uzbek and English explaining what should be declared. We have to list all of our medication, our electronic equipment and all foreign currency. If a search finds we haven't declared everything we won't be admitted to Uzbekistan.

Back at the office the customs officers are sitting at a desk watching something on a visitor's iPhone. We've been told stories of files on phones and computers being searched for anything they find unacceptable. They are eating pumpkin seeds and spitting the husks onto the dusty floor. They couldn't be more uninterested.

Eventually the boss, a fat, sweaty man, drags himself away from the video and asks to see my medication. I get the bag off the bike and a younger official who speaks English goes through the bag. My herbal sleeping tablets spark a little interest that wanes when I explain what they are. My other medication is clearly marked and he seems happy with that. He circles the list of foreign currency, stamps the form and gives it back to me. That's it. I'm done and we've been here only about half an hour.

Brian: Processing the bike is taking much longer. The young man is very friendly and wants to talk about the bike and our trip. He's intrigued by Damien's sidecar. He's in no hurry and I learnt a long time ago – don't rush the officials. It doesn't make them go any faster.

We need to put our intended route on the paperwork. This means working out which border we will use when we leave Uzbekistan. I get out the paper map and spread it out on the ledge outside the office. We're going into Tajikistan and some of the borders are open only to locals, not foreigners. The official isn't sure which ones we can use so I don't know how we are expected to choose – not yet anyway. The young Uzbek man just shrugs and writes down a couple of towns. He's happy enough.

Shirley: The time for the bikes to be processed seems to be neverending. Every time I wander up Brian, Damien and the official are chatting. I can't be bothered trying to take part. A woman's view isn't called for and it's so hot I just want to rest.

I find a spot in the shade and watch the passengers from a minibus getting ready for the search of their belongings. They have boxes and bags and suitcases. There's containers of food and rolls of cloth – everything but the kitchen sink. Each item has to be opened and checked. I hope they're not in a hurry. This could take ages.

Finally, Brian brings the bike down for the customs search, my bag, of course. My medication is right on top and the official wants to know about it. He seems satisfied when I tell him it's already been checked. A quick look through the bag with our jumpers and we're right to go.

Brian: The minute we ride out we are surrounded by money changers. They are wearing scarves wrapped around the faces to keep the sand, that is being whipped up by the hot wind, out of their mouths and noses. Sunglasses protect their eyes. It's a very harsh environment. Before leaving Kazakhstan I checked the going rate for Rouble to the local Som and expect to be ripped off. The Internet rate is 45. The money changer offers us 63! It's a deal! They hand over a wad of money – 5000 som is worth about AUD$2.50.

The money changer directs us to the insurance office and follows us in. There's no chance of making the same mistake we made in Kazakhstan. I get a policy for 56,000 som using my leftover Kazak teng.

Locals on the road from Nukus to Khiva

A statue of medieval mathematician, al-Khwārizmī, Khiva

The old Silk Road, Khiva

Again the going rate is much higher than the official rate.

The insurance office sells cold drinks. They are welcome after the time spent in the heat inside the border. We sit in front of the fan, sipping cold water and Cokes waiting for Damien to sort out his finances and insurance.

•

It's 2pm and we still have about 350 kilometres to the next major centre – Nukus. We'd like to get there tonight because there may not be anything else on the highway.

The temperature is in the high 30s now and the going is slow. The roads haven't improved. There's very little out here except the odd mangy-looking camel and more of the massive cemeteries we saw in Kazakhstan. The drivers we do encounter give us plenty of room when they pass and give us the thumbs up of friendship. Like the Kazaks, they are incredibly friendly – not at all reserved like the Russians.

Shirley: I need a break so we pull into a roadside café cum motel cum mechanical repair shop. Men are working on buses and trucks and there are a couple of small vans on the dusty forecourt. It's cooler in the café but it's filthy. People have obviously been having their lunch. Their plates are piled up on the counter with food scraps and the flies are having a ball. I need to go to the toilet. I'm hoping they have inside plumbing but I'm directed outside.

I can smell the toilets before I see them. There's a brick wall blocking the view from the road and I can hear the flies buzzing. I've never seen such a disgusting toilet. The flies, the stench – I nearly gag. I hang on.

Back in the café they ask if we'd like a room or something to eat. No thanks.

We ride on and it's getting hotter and dustier. After about another hour we see a sign for a café on the edge of an industrial town. Damien and I go in to get a cold drink. While we are in the shop a young man tells Brian they have rooms for US$40 per night. Brian thinks it's too expensive and gets ready to gear up and get moving.

Nukus is still 100 kilometres away, a long way on such a hot afternoon. Damien and I are both shagged so we go looking for the man touting the rooms. He tells us his family has come from Korea to start up this business. They plan to open a Korean restaurant in the motel. For the time being the café is serving meals all day.

The rooms are clean and have modern air-conditioning units. There's a shared bathroom with a couple of shower stalls and three squat toilets – all immaculately clean. It might be expensive but majority rules. We take two rooms and our passports are taken to register us with the local police.

•

The café's kitchen has a wall of glass showing a clean workspace with at least 10 people cooking in woks, fryers and grills. Truck drivers, workers from a nearby plant, are all hoeing into plates piled high with Korean food, washing it down with bottles of beer or whisky. The food is delicious. It's the best meal we've had for days and we seem to be in the middle of nowhere at a roadside stop.

•

Tomorrow we plan to visit the Aral Sea, or where the Aral Sea used to be. We could ride there from here or move on to Nukus and ride from there. That's a decision for the morning.

Brian: I'm glad Shirl and Damien won last night. I've slept soundly on clean sheets in a cool room. I'm ready for anything today can throw at us.

It makes sense to stay another night here and spend the day at the Aral Sea. The Korean family is happy to go back to the police and re-register us.

•

We go to Kungrad, the nearest town, to fuel up. The first two service stations we find are serving gas only. That's a problem here. Most of the cars run on gas, which is produced locally, not petrol. The only petrol we can find is 80 RON. The bike doesn't like it too much but it keeps running.

•

We ride the 100 odd kilometres to Moynaq, once a thriving Aral Sea fishing village and now a sandy, desolate town more than 120 kilometres from the shoreline. In 1960 the water lapped on the edge of the village and the fishing fleet kept hundreds of people in work. By 2000 it was gone. Russia pumped water out of the Aral Sea to create cotton crops in the desert, ignoring the environmental impact of this stupid use of water.

An ancient madrassa, Khiva

Eating like the locals, Khiva

The ancient city of Khiva at sunset

Today rusting ships of all shapes and sizes are stranded on what was once the seabed. It is a sobering sight. Standing on a cliff that now looks down on nothing but sand as far as the eye can see, it's hard to imagine cool water and the hustle and bustle of fishermen unloading their catch.

We are not the only visitors. Six women, old friends from Russia, Kazakhstan and Uzbekistan on holiday, arrive in a minibus. They have a driver and a videographer who is recording their holiday. We become part of it. Their laughter is contagious. They swarm around me and Damien, posing for photos around the bikes. Damien jokes that he could easily find a wife here – if he didn't already have one at home in Canada!

Shirley: The temperature has climbed to well over 40°C. There's a little store in town that seems to be the centre of the community. It sells everything from icy cold drinks to bolts of fabric, toys, clothing. It's like a miniature department store. The only thing of interest to us are the cold drinks.

A little red Suzuki 4x4 turns up and two very red-faced, fair skinned foreigners get out. They are from Ireland and decided, for something different, they would drive to Mongolia. I tell them I'm so jealous of their air-conditioned car.

'Oh, it's not air-conditioned. We didn't think it would be this hot.'

Really?

We talk about their trip and they're interested in ours. Damien is unusually quiet. When they leave he asks me if they were speaking English. He couldn't understand a word they were saying!

•

We need fuel and money so we head to Nukus, hoping we can get 91 or 95 RON fuel rather than the 80 that's been available so far, and find a bank that will let us withdraw money using our credit cards. This is the first country we've ridden through on this trip where there are very few ATMs and those that do exist don't take foreign cards.

On the way we are passed by a van with some kind of challenge advertised on the side. They pull up for a chat. They're from Scotland and are competing in a charity drive to Mongolia. We'll probably bump into them again along the way. They do have air-conditioning!

Nukus is a large city and I know from the minute we start looking for a bank that this isn't going to be easy. The GPS directs us to one alongside the 'White House', a government building. Brian finds a bit of shade and Damien and I trudge off in the heat to get some cash. This bank is a head office – no transactions here. The security guard directs us to another, just down the road. They refuse to help but they do give us the name of a bank that will and write that name on a slip of paper.

Trying to make our way there we get stopped by the police. I immediately ask if they know this bank, turning a check point into a cry for help. We get more directions to yet another bank where the story is the same. They can't help us, but they give us the name of yet another bank and a mud map. It is the National Bank. They must help us.

Tempers are fraying and Brian is getting really shitty. It's very hot again this morning and driving backwards and forwards around this city, contending with trucks, buses and cars isn't easy, so I can't really blame him.

We finally find the National Bank and it is alongside the first bank we visited. We have ridden around the entire city for more than an hour and we're back where we started. I really think Brian is going to explode. There's a road block stopping us from getting near the bank so Brian rides through the bollards and parks outside. I pity the poor security guard who tries to move him on from under the tree.

Damien and I go in and yet again we are told, by a man sitting in a small security box, that they can't help us. The usually even-tempered Damien loses it. He sticks his head in the man's window and gives it to him. The veins in his neck are standing out as he explains, through gritted teeth, how many banks we visited and how bad it is to treat visitors to Uzbekistan this way. Well done, Damien.

Needless to say it doesn't make any different to our predicament, but Damien feels a lot better after letting off steam. The guard is a little taken aback. When Damien is calmer he tells us we need the Kapital Bank which is just around the corner.

Brian just shakes his head in disbelief when I give him the news. We tear off and find the Kapital Bank in a leafy side street, well away from the business district. Inside the professional staff organise withdrawals of

Khiva at dusk

Kalta-minor minaret, Khiva

Getting to know the locals on road to Bukhara - check out the use of plastic bottles in the walls

Statue of the 'wise fool', Lyab-i Hauz, Bukhara

Poi Kalon, Bukhara

US dollars from our credit cards. A barrow boy a little way down the street is selling icy cold drinks. A couple of waters, a Coke and some nuts and all is calming down.

Luckily the GPS takes us straight to a petrol station that is selling better fuel, which saves a lot of angst.

Now we can hit the road for Khiva, an ancient city on the Silk Road, once the great trade route from China to the Mediterranean. The Silk Road was actually a series of roads that connected China with cities in Persia, North Africa and as far north as Russia. We are riding on the section through Uzbekistan but have ridden sections in India and Iran on earlier trips.

Brian: I can't believe the stuffing around just to get some cash. It's good to be on the road, out of the city until we get to an intersection on the highway patrolled by a cardboard cut-out of a police car. We turn off the main road for what looks like a more direct route.

This proves to be a huge mistake. It is the same as the worst roads we've be on and it's slow going.

We ride across a 300-metre long floating bridge over a river. It creaks and moans and every section moves underneath the weight of the bikes. It's an unnerving experience.

The road might be bad but the scenery is more interesting than kilometre after kilometre of sand. There are rice paddies, cotton fields, boys on donkeys towing carts laden with bales of cotton so big you can't see around them and old men pedalling bicycles slowly along the road.

By the time we get to Khiva it's after 5pm. We've spent eight hours on the road today, in temperatures reaching 40°C and higher.

I don't have the GPS coordinates for the hotel but it's called the Old Khiva hotel so I head to the old city. There it is, right across the road from the old city wall, a massive sandy coloured mud-wall that looks like it hasn't changed for centuries. It's a relief to get to the end of the day.

Shirley: The boys are chilling out in the front garden with a cold beer while I check out our room. It's clean, has a double bed and a western toilet – I'm a happy girl!

The going rate for the US dollar to the Uzbek som is 2574. The hotel manager gives us 4300. Clearly the black market is the way to change money here.

We head out for dinner around 8pm, as the sun sets. The city is cast in a beautiful light. The minarets with their turquoise tiles, the domes of the mosques and the madrassas (the Islamic religious schools) are all just gorgeous in the soft light of sunset.

We dine under the trees in an outdoor restaurant, lazing back on day beds, resting on masses of exquisite cushions. The kebabs, rice and bread – perfect. The local white wine is served chilled and by the glass. It is incredibly good. I had no idea there was a local wine. Apparently it is exported to Russia and other Central Asian countries.

We walk back through the narrow streets of the old city. It is very peaceful and the evening air is cool. I have fallen in love with Khiva.

•

My love for this city deepens when we see it through the eyes of a local guide, Izzat. University educated, he comes from a small village near here and knows and understands every laneway and square in Khiva. Izzat brings this oasis between two deserts to life. Legend has it that the town was founded by the son of Noah after he discovered a well here. Over the centuries it has been invaded, with the Russians taking over in the 1700s. This morphed into Soviet rule until independence in 1991.

Over the years much has been done to restore and maintain the beautiful buildings of Khiva. Possibly the most spectacular is what is now known as the Museum of Pillars. It was once a mosque, its roof supported by more than 200 carved wooden pillars. Inside there is a peaceful garden with mulberry trees. They were planted here because their roots spread out, absorbing much of the moisture that could damage the wooden pillars.

Izzat leads us through the tiled mosques and madrassas, into the tiny 'cells' where students studied the Koran, the harem and reception halls. If only the walls could share their stories of the political intrigues over the centuries. Some of the ornate mausoleums are now locations for wedding photos. Brides hope that the wisdom of the men who lie here will pass on to their sons.

We look out over the old city from the ramparts. The heat haze

Chos Bakr, Bukhara

Sultan and Darlia at the Chos Minor Hotel, Bukhara

Regastan Square, Samarkand

shimmers on the tiled domes and minarets.

Our tour ends at the mausoleum of a wrestler who showed the leader how to be righteous, caring and save lives by thinking outside of the square. It's an extra cost but worth the 5000 – the tile work is incredible and locals come here to pray. The brides are here – the wrestler was obviously a very wise man with much to offer the future of Uzbekistan.

It's 2pm and too hot to walk around. The streets are deserted, with the cool restaurants the place to be. Aubergine and Somsa, the local dumplings – delicious.

Brian: There is a mural map of the Silk Road outside the main city gates, showing the road weaving across Persia, India, Central Asia and Europe. A French biker is there taking a photo of himself and his bike with the map. He's just come out of Tajikistan, the next stage of our journey. We've heard there's been a massive landslide. He missed it by just 100 metres. The road is closed and people are suffering. That could mean a change of plans for us.

•

Damien goes overland to get the sidecar into the square so we can get our photo of the bikes with the Silk Road map. The bollards, presumably set up to prevent such activity, pose a problem but he gets around them.

No matter how hard we try, we never hit the road early. It's 9.30am before we are on the road to Bukhara, another ancient town on the Silk Road. It's getting hot already.

The roads have been appalling since we left Russia. Each day has tossed up bad roads, worse roads and, very occasionally, reasonable roads. Today is no different until we hit a 140-kilometre stretch of perfectly sealed, brand new highway. It ends as abruptly as it begins, without any warning signs. It was nice while it lasted.

Our first stop of the day is to record a momentous occasion. Our motorcycle ticks over 200,000 kilometres. Now, that's an achievement. Big Red is showing no signs of slowing down.

As the heat soars and the road gets bad again we stop for a break at a roadside café in the middle of nowhere. The owner has cold water, frozen water and cold Coke. We get one of each. The kitchen is closed but he will cook some Manti for us – another form of dumpling, similar to the Somsa we had in Khiva. He offers to serve the food in his air-conditioned room, where we can rest. We opt to sit under the trees in the garden. I might not get Shirl out of an air-conditioned room.

Three children appear and watch us eat, giggling behind their hands. They're sitting on a wall made of plastic drink bottles cemented together. It's a constructive way of recycling the ubiquitous plastic bottle.

We can't delay the inevitable and hit the road again. More bad roads, closed petrol stations or petrol stations that have no fuel at all. One boasts a sign saying they have 95 RON. The motorcycle needs some good fuel, but the bowser isn't working, of course. Apparently there is a service station with 92 RON, 22 kilometres down the road. When we get there, they are out of fuel altogether. Thank goodness for the 33-litre adventure tanks. We both have enough fuel to get to Bukhara.

Shirley: Looks can be deceiving and our hotel in Bukhara is a perfect example. Tucked in a narrow, dusty road, the *Chor Minor* hotel, named after the unique madrassa with four minarets around the corner, looks pretty rundown from the outside but inside it is bright, airy and decorated in the local style with Moorish artwork and rooms built around an atrium that lets in loads of natural light. On each level there is a little sitting area. In our room there is a tray of delightful Uzbek sweets, nuts and fine toffee swirls. All this for only US$60.

Sultan, the owner, speaks four languages but not English. His receptionist, Dalia, speaks pretty good English and welcomes us. Sultan shows Brian to a house around the corner that has a locked yard. The road is too narrow for Damien's sidecar, but our bike will stay there. There is a dog with a small puppy living in the yard. She doesn't like her area being disrupted and bites Brian. Thank goodness his bike pants are thick enough to resist the attempt to protect her baby.

Damien's sidecar is slowly falling apart because of the terrible road conditions. He needs to do a bit of work on it, replacing broken bolts. Sultan makes some calls and organises for Damien to go to a workshop tomorrow and fix all the little niggling problems.

Damien and I are standing outside our rooms, talking, when Sultan motions for me to put my shoes on. At first I think he doesn't like bare

Shah-i-Zhinda
mausoleums,
Samarkand

Mausoleum of Gur Emir - Tamerlane, Samarkand

feet in the hotel but then I realise he wants us to follow him up the stairs. He opens a little door and we walk out onto the hotel's roof. The sun is setting over Bukhara — its domes, minarets and the *Chor Minor* behind us. It is the most magnificent sight. We are looking out on history. It is breathtaking.

We walk back down and Sultan has laid out some watermelon on a low table surrounded by cushions. It is a fine gesture of friendship and welcome.

•

Around 8pm we head out to find somewhere to eat. We are literally five minutes from *Lyab-i Hauz* — an ancient plaza with a pool at its centre. Under centuries old mulberry trees there is a fantastic restaurant. It is a peaceful place, even though the restaurant is busy.

Around the plaza are two ancient madrassas - *Nodir Divan-begi* on one side and Khanaka Nodir-Divan begi on the other. They are lit, highlighting the tilework that adorns them.

Conversation turns to how hard the ride has been over the past few days. It is amazing how revitalised we all feel after a shower, putting on some fresh clothes and sitting down with a cold drink and some food.

We feel blessed to be sitting here, in the middle of an historic Silk Road town with Damien. We've known each other for only a few days but we are developing a deep friendship. There's only one thing missing, Damien's wife, Sylvie. I know he is missing her and being with us must make her absence even tougher.

•

As well as being a major stop on the Silk Road, Bukhara was the centre of Islamic studies during medieval times. That explains the number of madrassas, mosques, bazaars and caravanserais that we will explore tomorrow.

Brian: The long hot days on the road are taking their toll. We're all glad to have a sleep in. Breakfast is set out for us. There's goats cheese, cream that you eat with jam and bread, cheese, melon and an egg with tomato. It's pretty damn good.

Sultan has hooked Damien up with a local lad who speaks English. He is taking him to a workshop and will act as interpreter so the sidecar can get the TLC it desperately needs. The boy is delighted. He gets to sit in the sidecar for the ride, something that will give him bragging rights with his friends.

Shirl and I go into the town, soaking up the atmosphere. We get the feeling that nothing much has changed here over the past couple of centuries. The buildings have been well preserved and beautifully restored. Even the modern hotels have been sympathetically designed to blend in with the older buildings.

We walk through a bazaar selling beautiful handicrafts, exquisitely embroidered bags, knives with intricately carved handles, chess sets, scarves, jewellery. Shirl is a pretty good shopper and she is a master at working out how to use local postal systems. Unfortunately for her I've been told all post from the 'Stans' goes through Russia. After the hassle we had with the parcel in Moscow there is no way I'm going through that again. Whatever she buys here we have to carry.

Around every corner we see the *Kalon* Minaret towering above the buildings. Built in the 10th Century it was once the tallest structure in all of Central Asia. It stands 47 metres tall, with incredibly deep foundations that have stood the test of time, surviving many earthquakes. It is covered in glazed blue tiles and shines like a beacon above the town.

Next to it is the *Kalon* Mosque with its equally spectacular bright blue domes, shimmering in the harsh sunlight. This is again a place of worship, after years of being used as a grain store during the Soviet era.

•

As the day wears on the heat becomes unbearable. We find a cool spot by the *Lyab-i Hauz* pool and take a break before heading back to meet Damien. On the way we bump into a biker from the UK. He's heading to China via Tajikistan's Pamir Highway and has heard the road is closed. I'll keep checking. Hopefully we can get through.

Damien is despondent. While he was getting the bike fixed his iPod has gone missing. He's not sure if he lost it or if it's been stolen. He has stored a lot of photos on it and it's the way he contacts Sylvie when he has the Internet.

Shirl gives him a big hug. She's mothering him but I think he appreciates it. There are times a hug is just what you need.

Tamerlane, Samarkand   Mausoleum of Gur Emir - Tamerlane, Samarkand

Sweet treats – Samarkand Market

Powdered tobacco – Samarkand Market

Shirley: After a rest Damien feels a lot brighter. He's going to offer a reward in the hope the iPod finds its way back to him. Dalia is taking us out for a traditional Uzbek dinner tonight and we'll stop at the tourist police office on the way so Damien can report the theft.

I don't know what we are expecting for the venue of our traditional dinner, but it's not the concrete yard surrounded by a brick wall Dalia takes us to. The food is plentiful and tasty, but not that exotic – just kebabs with salad and rice.

Dalia suggests we walk home. It's a long walk through the newer part of the city in the dark over uneven footpaths. We pass a massive hotel that is in darkness. It has been built but there are not enough visitors to warrant opening it.

In the main square the fountain is lit with the most vibrant purples, reds and blues. The water dances and children are having a fun time playing 'chicken' with the spouts. The most popular activity for the younger kids is a ride in a remote controlled car. Adults have the controls which is just as well. There are so many of them there'd be a major traffic jam.

When we get near Dalia's home, on the edge of the old city, she bids us goodnight and tells us to 'go straight'. This is going well until we get to a 'V' shaped junction and we're not sure which lane would be going straight. We take a guess and end up just at the end of our street. More good luck than good management!

•

After another day wandering the streets of this wonderful city we get a table by the pool at *Lyab-i Hauz*. At a nearby table there are four foreign backpackers. Their conversation is so loud it is impossible to ignore. Two Russian girls are telling the two young American men that the countries of the west are frightened of Vladimir Putin. They talk about the international press lying about their great leader and their country, particularly the Russian involvement in the downing of the Malaysian airliner over the Ukraine last year. Scores of Australians were killed and this morning I read a moving piece in an Australian online newspaper about the sunflowers at the crash site being preserved for the families of the dead. It was a moving piece and I'm not in the mood to listen to the young, ill-informed Russians. I tell Brian we have to leave. I can't guarantee that I won't head over to their table and tell them a few home truths. Mind you, I'm sure they'd just think of me as a crazy old Australian who doesn't know what she's talking about. Sometimes it's better to just shut up, especially as we've been told not to discuss politics with Russians.

•

I calm down and we had back to *Lyab-i Hauz* for our last night in Bukhara. A cold beer, a glass of wine and some Somsa – perfect.

Brian: We are moving on to Samarkand, another historic town. The road is remarkably good, so when Damien disappears from my mirrors I'm surprised. We pull over under a tree, where some very industrious children have set up an old freezer and are selling cold drinks, to wait for him.

Shirl buys a bottle and is leaning against the bike when one of the children comes up and speaks to us. We have no idea what he is saying, but he's pointing into a ditch under the trees where the children have some old car seats set up.

When we don't move, his sister drags up one of the old seats for Shirl. She then goes back and drags another one up on to the roadside and sits down with Shirl. It is such a lovely gesture. They are obviously intrigued by the foreigners on the motorcycle and would love to talk to us. The language barrier is a curse at times like this.

I'm getting very worried about Damien and I'm about to head back to find him when he appears on the highway. The repairs made on the sidecar have given out and part of the rack has fallen off completely and is now strapped onto the sidecar.

The only thing he has to say is, 'I lost my iPod for nothing.'

Poor Damien. He can't take a trick at the moment.

•

Our hotel is in a small street just off the main road into town. To get to it there is a long pathway between two buildings – too narrow for a car, a tight squeeze for the sidecar but perfect for our bike. This is the best spot to keep the bikes safe for the next couple of days while we explore Samarkand, said to be the most beautiful of the Silk Road cities. It's got a lot to beat. We've all loved Khiva and Bukhara.

•

Heading out to dinner we find ourselves in a rabbit warren of narrow laneways at the back of a large mosque. We make a turn that takes us into an even narrower lane. There's no sign of a restaurant or even a store so we turn back and head to the main street on the other side of the hotel. There's a chicken shop – that will do.

Walking in it's pretty obvious they don't get too many foreigners here. The chatter from the diners ceases and all eyes turn to us in the doorway. It's reminiscent of the bar scene in the Star Wars movie. They check us all out and then go back to their meals. At one table there's a group of women, dressed as if they are going out to the Ritz, counting wads of currency. They are not trying to hide the huge amounts of money. At another table a man has obviously been enjoying the whisky rather than the chicken and has to be helped out. Even though this is a Muslim country alcohol is readily available, but this is the first man we've seen who's been over-refreshed. Scattered around the large restaurant are family groups who keep telling the children to turn around and stop staring at us. It's not a problem, we're used to being the centre of attention in this part of the world.

Shirley: Damien's not feeling too well today but he's determined to get out and see Samarkand. We've organised a guide to show us around and head off on foot to the area we headed towards last night. If we'd turned left instead of right we would have been in the heart of the bazaar and in front of the most magnificent mosque, its minaret and dome covered in the beautiful tile work that is the trademark of the area.

Alexander, our guide, is a short man with bundles of energy. He is keen to keep us moving but there is so much to see in the bazaar. The tobacco section sells powdered tobacco of varying quality and taste. The locals put it under their tongues. It's sold by the gram and is served in a pear-shaped container that has its own little brush to dust the tobacco residue off your hand.

There are eggs of all shapes and sizes, vegetables and fruit but it's the sweets that get my attention. Honey and sugar made into a light, sweet toffee and nougat with pistachio nuts, a favourite from our visit to Iran – delicious.

It seems like around every corner and at the end of every laneway there are mosques and madrassas, all now public monuments rather than places of worship and study. Alexander tells us stories of growing up in the city during the years of Soviet rule when religion was not encouraged. Today there are small working mosques on the outskirts of the city and Alexander believes that one day some of these major mosques will need to be used for prayer again. As the years pass the number of people practising their religion grows, he says.

The buildings are superb and there are so many of them it's impossible to absorb it all – history overload.

Alexander loves his city and is proud of the way it has been restored over the years. He remembers watching masses of people in bazaars in what are now courtyards in mosque forecourts and workers carrying out the painstaking restoration work, retiling minarets and domes.

Samarkand's favourite son is Timur or Tamerlane as he's better known. They worship him and have forgiven or forgotten the millions of people he killed as he plundered his way across Asia in the 1300s. He planned to reopen the Silk Road with Samarkand at its heart. He died on his way to take China. Today his likeness looks down on a major intersection and people still pray at his mausoleum.

The jewel in the crown of Samarkand is the Registan, the commercial centre of the city in medieval times. The square is surrounded by picture-perfect madrassas that are the finest examples of the bright blue tile work. There are lecture halls, tiny cells once used by students now selling handicrafts, and what was once a massive mosque, built in the time of Tamerlane. The tile work on some of the interiors feature Arabic calligraphy. Some are inlaid with gold. We sit to absorb the history and beauty that is before us. It is breathtaking.

Over lunch Alexander talks about the Soviet times and hints that all is not so much better today, under the current president. I ask when the next election might be. Alexander answers, 'Only God knows.' He explains that at the last election every candidate supported the president. That is an interesting take on democracy.

Our last stop is at *Shah-i-Zinda*, the avenue of mausoleums. The tile work here is said to be some of the best in the Muslim world. It is unsurpassed in beauty. A cousin of the Prophet Mohammad is buried here. So is Tamerlane's sister. Their status is recognised by the quality of the decoration work. The colours are vibrant and the intricate work a testament to the craftsmen. Much of it has needed little or no restoration.

•

Back at the hotel there is a surprise for Damien. His iPod is here! Sultan drove all the way from Bukhara to deliver it personally. What an incredible thing to do. It's such a long drive. He had already left to return home by the time we got back from our day exploring the city. Damien never finds out where it had been or how Sultan came to get it back but there a pictures of a young family stored on it. A mystery that is not solved.

Brian: Shirl is crook today – one of the lesser joys of travelling through this part of the world. The water, the food – many things, can leave you with an upset tummy and worse. I'm sure it wasn't the food from the delightful restaurant we ate at last night, sitting on a terrace overlooking Registan. The kebabs were delicious, much better than the roast chook the night before.

•

Carlo, a 60-something Italian travel agent is driving around Central Asia looking for tour opportunities to offer back home. He and his friend, Pietro, are in a four-wheel drive and have a young Uzbek woman as their guide and interpreter. She speaks fluent Italian, but very little English.

They've just come through Tajikistan and the Pamir region. The road that skirts the Afghanistan border is open and he says we will get through as long as we take our time. The main highway is still blocked by the landslide, so the trucks are going through the Pamir and that is causing some problems, but he's really positive about our chances of getting through.

Shirl emerges from our room just as Carlo invites us all to lunch. Their guide is taking them to a local restaurant that only serves Plov cooked the traditional way. *Plov* is the speciality of Central Asia and we actually haven't tasted it yet. It's basically a pilaf – rice, vegetables and sometimes meat.

The six of us jam into Carlo's car and head out into the suburbs to the restaurant. Outside there are police and a huge crowd. A car has somehow driven off the road and is upside down on the walkway below road level – right at the door to the restaurant. The lunchtime crowd isn't deterred and nor are we. We squeeze past the wrecked car and into the restaurant.

It is an enormous space with a small open courtyard in the centre.

Cashed up – US$50 goes a long way

Damien and Brian take tea, Samarkand

We say goodbye to Damien on the road to Tashkent

There's seating for a couple of hundred at tables for 10 and more. Most of the diners are men, with a couple of groups of foreigners with their guides.

The food is very tasty and there's plenty of it. We're offered the local yogurt drink but pass on that. A cold beer is the perfect accompaniment to this local staple. Shirl passes on both but seems to enjoy the *Plov*.

•

Back at the hotel there's a Swiss-registered bike. Gio, an Irishman now living in Switzerland, is heading to Tajikistan tomorrow. We'll probably ride with him to the border.

•

It's our last night with Damien. Instead of going into Tajikistan he's continuing on through Uzbekistan, heading to Mongolia. He has a date with his wife in Ulaanbaatar, the Mongolian capital.

For our last supper we go to the Samarkand Restaurant recommended by the hotel owner. There's a dress regulation of no shorts but that doesn't seem to apply to foreigners. Just as well as Damien, Gio and I all have shorts on. The place is rocking. There's a wedding in the main part of the restaurant and the band is belting out dance tunes. Children are running about, beautiful women are dancing beside their tables, trying to entice their men to join them.

The steaks are massive and really good. I notice Shirl is just pushing her chicken and rice around on her plate. I guess she's still not feeling so good.

Shirley: I'm sorry to be leaving Damien. He, like Dave, has been a good travelling companion and we've shared some funny times and seen some incredible sights together. He's heading to Tashkent and we'll cross into Tajikistan today.

Paying our hotel bill ends up being a real stuff up. The credit card machine needs Wi-Fi to work. Today is August 1 and the Internet ticks over to a new billing cycle today. It doesn't reboot until midday so there's no access to the credit facility until then. Pity they didn't mention this last night.

Using the last of my US dollars I manage to pay our bill but I will have to borrow some som from Gio to buy fuel.

•

Brian and Gio have no trouble getting their bikes out of the hotel garden and into the passageway. It's not so easy for Damien and the sidecar. Brian and Gio are pushing the rig up the couple of steps when I see my boy leap back with a pained expression on his face.

He's torn the calf muscle in his left leg. He heard it go. This is not the start we needed today. We are about to embark on what could be a very difficult part of the trip.

•

We get to the intersection with the main road to Tashkent. It's time to say goodbye to Damien. I'm sad and it's made worse because I know Damien is going to be lonely, travelling on his own again.

We hug and kiss. He and Brian embrace until Damien points out that in France men kiss too. They embrace again and kiss on the cheeks.

There is a bond between travellers and this cements it.

We've experienced the best and the worst of overland travel together riding through Kazakhstan and Uzbekistan.

We hope to meet up again – somewhere on the road.

Tajikistan

1 – 13 August

Shirley: I feel sad as I watch Damien ride off, but we have more roads to travel. Gio is with us, heading for the Tajikistan border. Brian has one road keyed into the GPS that Gio thinks is only for locals. Rather than telling Brian he's wrong we all ride together.

The border is closed to foreigners. There's no 'I told you so' from Gio. He just suggests we follow him to the next border, only 35 kilometres away.

The first person we meet at the border is the money changer. I get US$100 worth of Tajik somoni. He gives us the same exchange rate as the XE website rates. There's no black market here. I always feel better when I have some local currency in my pocket.

We're pushed to the top of the queue at the border post and are presented with the departure forms to fill in. I make sure I list the foreign currency we have and that it is less than we arrived with. At some ATMs in Uzbekistan I was able to get US dollars but after the debacle when we paid our hotel bill this morning that is just about gone so I don't even need to fib on my form. I add the Tajik somoni and they ignore that.

The search of my bag is quite thorough this time which surprises me considering we are leaving the country. The guard forces his hand to the very bottom of my pannier and produces my Go Girl. He wants to know what it is. The Go Girl was a present from Brian just before we left home. It's a device that allows women to pee standing up. It's all well and good in theory but my bike pants have a waterproof skin inside the zip so I'd have to take them off to pee using the Go Girl anyway, that defeats the purpose. I'm not sure how to describe its purpose to the guard so I just say 'for women'. He gets very embarrassed, shoves it back into my pannier and tells me to shut the bag.

•

On the Tajik side the paperwork is simple. We fill in the immigration form and we're let in the gate. The friendly guards stamp our passports and direct us to the customs shed. The bikes are parked to one side and we're ushered into an air-conditioned office where the officials do the paperwork for the bike. There is a fee of US$10 for the bike. We pay it and get a receipt so we know we are not contributing to someone's holiday fund, which isn't always the case. Sometimes officials ask for 'fees' that go into the bottom drawer.

Outside this area there's a pool of disinfectant of some kind we have to ride through. That done we're officially in Tajikistan. As we head out of the border an official shouts, 'welcome to Tajikistan'.
Thanks.

•

Our first Tajik petrol station has 95 RON fuel, which is a very good start to this part of our journey. There is a small shop attached and the boys working there are delighted to give me a guided tour of all they have to offer. There's pretty good-looking fruit and vegetables and plenty of packet goods, but all we really need is a cold drink.

Outside the owner appears with a huge watermelon for us and a honeydew melon for Gio. With deepest apologies we decline this kind gesture. He is disappointed we can't accept his gifts, but neither bike has any room to carry a melon. The scene reminds me of Ron Fellowes, an Australian who rode a vintage bike from Kathmandu to Belgium. His book is called *No Room for Watermelons*.

We say goodbye to Gio. His plans have changed so he's heading north rather than into the Pamir Region of Tajikistan. He has some pens and pencils he wanted to give the children in Mongolia and asks us to take them for him. There's not much room on the bike but we squeeze them in.

Brian's leg is our only problem. He doesn't say too much, but I can tell he's in a lot of pain and needs to rest. At Chkalovsk we find a hotel, a very modern building with a delightful garden and fountain in the backyard where the bike will be tucked away for the night. (According to reports online the Tajikistan government has since decided to change the name of Chkalovsk to Buston so it doesn't sound so Russian.)

When we get into our room Brian gets out of his bike gear to reveal

Dushanbe

We talked our way out of a speeding fine

Propaganda posters

Khaburabot Pass

a badly swollen calf muscle. He lies down for a rest and instantly falls asleep. I hope he is not getting sick. That is the last thing we need.

Brian: My leg is really sore but I feel a bit better after a good night's sleep. The owner of the hotel pops into the room to welcome us and apologises for not coming to see us last night. I'm glad he didn't.

He helps bring our luggage down and I load up the bike out the front of the hotel with only a small audience. After the obligatory photo he presents us with a small ceramic jug and plate to welcome us to his country. Shirl wraps them in her clothes in the top of the pannier to keep them safe. I don't think I can even fit a cigarette paper on the bike now!

He also has some advice for us about the road to Dushanbe.

'It is good apart from one seven-kilometre tunnel. That will be dark and have water in it. I suggest you take the route over the pass. The scenery is very nice.'

I've heard about the tunnel – dubbed the 'Tunnel of Death' or the 'Tunnel of Fear'. It bypasses the Anzob Pass. Built by the Iranians, it is dangerous. Water constantly runs through the tunnel and this hides the potholes that may be shallow or deep. They may be just a hole or they may be disguising sharp bits of steel reinforcing from the road.

I don't have to look at Shirl to know she's not happy about the prospect of a ride through the tunnel. Friends who travelled this road last year told us it was awful but they lived to tell the tale and I'm sure we will too.

•

The road to Dushanbe is very good and we're making excellent time. The mountain roads are letting me enjoy the bike for a change, rather than dodging the potholes on the Uzbek roads. I pull up at a tea house in a valley surrounded by trees. It is cool spot for a break. I order some of the local soup but Shirl hasn't got an appetite for anything other than the plainest foods. She has a packet of Pringles potato chips and a Coke. I hope she gets her appetite back soon. It's not like her to knock back food.

•

Rested and revived we head back out. Riding down farther into the valley the road starts to deteriorate, getting worse and worse. The trees disappear and the scenery is just rocks, sand and dust. There are so many trucks on the road we are constantly covered in dust, clambering over broken road, holes, gravel and sand, it is hard work. It just goes on and on.

We get to an intersection where we can head up but it is blocked by the police. This is the entrance to the 'Tunnel of Death' and it's closed. I'm not sure whether that's a good thing or a bad thing. Surely it couldn't be any worse than what we are riding through now.

The going is so slow, but finally we come down out of the mountains and into a verdant valley. All around us are snow-capped mountains. It is incredibly beautiful.

We're still about 100 kilometres from Dushanbe, the capital of Tajikistan and our overnight spot, but at least the road is better now and the air clear. We've left the choking dust behind us.

The city traffic is manic but even this doesn't seem so bad after battling the trucks, holes and dirt in the mountains.

Shirley: On the way to the hotel we ride past two of Dushanbe's major tourist attractions – the world's tallest flagpole and the statue of Ismoil Somoni, the 10th Century leader of the country. I know better than to ask Brian to stop after the ride we've had.

Today's shower is probably the most needed of the trip so far. It feels good to wash the dirt of the road off and get into some clean clothes.

We head out just on dusk. The fountain outside the Ballet Theatre Is a sea of changing colours. The water is dancing to classical music piped around the square. There are family groups enjoying the cooler night air and the spectacle of the light and sound show. It is as much fun watching the kids dancing and lovers walking around the fountain holding hands, as it is watching the show itself.

I'm feeling hungry, which is an incredibly good sign. We wander up a side street and find the Moscow Café. It is an outdoor restaurant with tables set around a fountain. The woman who seems to be the boss sits at a table near ours keeping a constant eye on all the staff and the guests, making sure everyone is enjoying themselves. Her English is pretty much non-existent but she hovers around us, smiling.

One of the waiters speaks English and he is sent to serve us. With his help, my Russian phrasebook and the *Picture Talk* book we order

Kids want to high-5 us

Kids showing off for the camera

The rugged road through the Pamir region

shashlik with salad. I'm taking a punt that the water is OK here. Brian orders a beer and I ask for a whisky and Coke. The whisky comes in a little glass jug with the Coke on the side. Perfect.

Maybe Tajikistan will be a good food destination!

•

I want to explore and Brian wants to rest his leg. It's very swollen now but he suffers in silence so I can see some of Dushanbe. First stop is the bank. It offers somoni and US dollars. We get a bit of both. US dollars come in very handy with money changers and some shop keepers prefer them to the local currencies.

We wander up the main boulevard, a wide, tree-lined street with some fine buildings from the Soviet era with their columns and elaborate porticos. It's hot and I'm not being fair to Brian expecting him to hike around the city so we head back to the hotel to rest.

The bike gear is putrid, covered in the grime of three months on the road. Armed with a bucket of hot, soapy water I lay the gear out on the grass in the hotel garden and scrub away. The housekeeper comes out and wants to do it for me. In the end we work away together with no common language but we laugh and smile as the grime washes away.

•

Brian's arranged to meet Bill, a Canadian biker, and his mates who are heading into the Pamir region, tonight. He doesn't know anything about Bill other than he's riding with a few friends, heading to the Pamir and hopefully getting all the way through to Magadan in Russia.

When two bikes pull up we know it's them. They are both about our age but rather than wearing bike pants and jackets they're in shorts and T-shirts with protective motorcycle armour. It's an odd look. Their hotel is only 10 minutes walk away. I can't work out why they didn't walk. Each to his own.

They haven't found a good place to eat in town so they're happy to try the Moscow Café. You'd think we were long-lost family members the way we are greeted when we walk in. The owner comes rushing over to us and envelops me in her arms. It's quite a welcome.

The food is good and so is the conversation. Bill and Michael will be heading down into the Pamir region tomorrow. The main road is still closed due to the landslide so they're heading to the road we plan to ride, that parallels the Afghanistan border. The way they're talking they'll be travelling quicker than us and camping whenever they feel they've had enough riding for the day. We'll probably stay in guesthouses, that are said to be everywhere in the Pamir.

While we're talking another bike pulls up and a long-haired, bearded man walks up and asks if we speak English. Brian goes to shake his hand and he winces. He explains, after telling us his name is Mihai, that he came off his bike and sprained his wrist. He's ridden from Romania and is heading to the Pamir too. We might meet some friendly faces down there.

Before we leave I convince the owner of the restaurant to join us in a photo. She won't smile. Photos are obviously very serious business here.

Brian: Today we leave for the Pamir and a ride into the unknown. Today the GPS decides not to work. There are two roads to the Pamir. One is said to be sealed all the way but is a lot longer than the main road – the M41. Without the GPS the M41 is going to be the easier to find because it's the main road right outside our hotel. This should be simple and it is, until I take a wrong turn and end up on some wonderful narrow back roads that take us through a hilly, rural area. It's one of those mistakes that ends up being well worth the detour. After a bit of back-tracking we end up on the M41 again and just keep on riding.

•

In a small village a policeman steps out in front of the bike and waves us down. He shows me the speed on the radar gun. We are doing 51 kilometres per hour in a 50 kilometre zone and the fine is 90 somoni. They've got to be kidding. This sounds like a donation rather than a fine to me.

We both get off the bike and Shirl gets out the Picture Talk book and the phrasebook. There's a lot of gesturing and head shaking. In the end they agree that we don't need to pay the fine. I think Shirl's charm and *Picture Talk* won them over. She ends up getting them to pose for a photo after agreeing to 'no Internet'.

The road has been good so far but once we get away from the police it begins to deteriorate. We're back to broken road surface, potholes and cracks. More of the same, with the odd shallow water crossing thrown in for good measure.

The serenity of a mountain pass in the Pamir region

The raging Panji River

Getting petrol, Kalaikhum

Cyclists in Kalaikhum on their way to China – and people say we're crazy

Shirley: Riding through small villages we keep hearing little voices calling out, 'Hello – Hello'. Sometimes we can see the boys swimming in a waterhole beside the road and waving at us. Or they are clambering over fences to get a glimpse of us. Those who can get onto the road run alongside the bike wanting to 'high 5' us. It's dangerous having them so close to the bike. If something happens and the bike swerves we could hit them and if we actually do make hand-to-hand contact it will hurt, even if we are only travelling at a slow speed. We try to dodge them. There's no shortage of smiling faces in every tiny village.

I'm starting to notice that even the smallest of the villages has a poster of their President displayed prominently. We first saw his image in the office at the Tajikistan Embassy in Vienna. That was just a portrait. Now we are seeing the man-of the people President. He's always wearing a suit. In some posters he is helping small children with their schoolwork. In others he has his jacket thrown casually over his arm and is strolling through a field of grain. He's obviously got a good PR machine.

There don't seem to be any hotels or guesthouses in most of the villages, just little mud houses with small vegetable gardens. There's plenty of cows, goats, sheep and donkeys, some with foals. We are moving away from the desert into an area with plenty of water, where the fields are green and lush with plenty of fodder for the animals.

We're heading into the Pamir Region, an area where admission is allowed only with a permit. It became an autonomous region during the Soviet times and remains that way today. The military and police man posts along the road, checking that we have the right paperwork. The guards don't have a lot to say for themselves. Well, they have nothing to say, really. And our Aussie charm doesn't even get them to smile. They are all pretty brusque.

At one, a group of children come up and introduce themselves. I repeat their names in my best Australian accent and they think it's hilarious.

The road takes us over the Khaburabot Pass. At more than 3000 metres the air is thin and cool, a pleasant change from the dry heat of the desert.

But it's desolate. We don't see anything or anyone, other than the odd goat herder in the pastures. They all wave as we ride past. It must be an incredibly isolated existence up here.

Coming down the other side we bump into three cyclists who are cycling to China – and people think we're crazy! Iain Fellowes and his companions have been camping for the past four nights and hope to make it to Kalaikhum, where there are a couple of guesthouses, tonight.

I feel really ill prepared for this part of the ride. I have no idea about the main towns and what accommodation is available.

I needn't have worried. The accommodation finds us. As we hit the edge of Kalaikhum a man steps out in front of the bike and asks if we want a hotel. He has a double room right over a raging river. The noise of the water is deafening. Lucky we have earplugs! The room has its own bathroom which is still under construction. The inner walls haven't been lined, there are nails sticking through from the other side and the toilet moves when you sit on it, but hey, it's a bathroom. The water runs hot and cold but for US$20 we are getting dinner, bed and breakfast. We think it's a good deal.

Brian: The cyclists take the other rooms and at dinner we're all joined by a young German couple who are staying at the other guesthouse in town. They're competing in the Mongolian charity run too. There must be a lot of foreigners around at the moment and we keep bumping into them on the road. The odd thing is we never see this couple again.

When it comes to food, Shirl and I are both pretty cautious. The chicken we're served for dinner seems undercooked so we both pass. The bread, tomato and onion and chips fill a gap. There are even some cold beers.

Earplugs in and we both sleep pretty well.

•

Loading the bike and Iain appears. He's crook, really crook. So are his mates. I guess it was the chicken, or it could have been the fact that they've been drinking the water from the streams when they camp for four days of living on two-minute noodles, followed by plenty of beer last night, upset them. They're going to stay here and rest. We're going south now, heading to Khorug.

We need to fuel up and have been told the petrol is on the other

Afghanistan is just across the river

Throwing a rock into Afghanistan, because I can

The trucks make a mess of the roads

The bike is standing on its own, bogged in sand

side of town. It's impossible to miss. The fuel truck is parked on the side of the road. On a table under an awning there are several metal jugs and a ladle and a 44-gallon drum. It's a simple process. The fuel is ladled from the drum into the jugs and then poured into the bike using a funnel. Thank goodness there are no smokers around!

The man serving the fuel is dressed in a pristine white shirt. He's quite short, much shorter than Shirl and has to stand on tiptoes and stretch to get the fuel into the funnel he's put into the tank.

•

It's another day of twisty roads, good roads, bad roads, gravel roads, sand, water and even some good pavement. The roads are taking us through the mountains. The Hindu Kush, Pamir and Himalaya all meet down here. The scenery is fantastic. The raging river and the snow-capped mountains nearly makes you forget the terrible condition of the road. I need to keep my wits about me.

At the edge of most of the villages there are checkpoints, officials always making sure that we have the right documentation to be in this part of the world. The road is hugging the Panji River that makes a natural border between Tajikistan and Afghanistan.

We come to a big water crossing and there are two SUVs ahead of us. One of them is stopped in the water. I'm pretty annoyed. There's just enough room for me to get around them but it's a stupid place to stop. As I'm about to take off I notice they have Australian number plates.

Shirl can't resist. As we pull alongside the second SUV she raises her visor and yells, 'Where did you get your licence?'

They recognise the Australian accent. They're from West Australia and are in the Mongolian Challenge charity run. It seems there are two charity runs heading to Mongolia. No wonder we keep bumping into foreigners on the road.

Shirley: I'm finding the going tough. Brian swerves around as many of the potholes as he can but he can't miss them all. We bump and crash into them, jarring us and the bike. It isn't doing any of us any good.
We've been told the place travellers stay in Khorug is the Pamir Lodge. This town is the capital of the region and there's plenty of markets, shops, even an expensive looking five-star hotel on the edge of town and a kiosk claiming to be a McDonalds outlet.

In town we meet Mika, a German riding a 350 Suzuki trail bike. He's trying to find the Pamir Lodge too. Eventually we get there, at the top of a dusty unmade road on the outskirts of the town. If this is the preferred option, I can't imagine what the rest of the guesthouses in town are like. There are no rooms left, but we can sleep on one of the beds on the verandah. The owner, a young woman who speaks pretty good English, tells me they have two showers and five toilets. This seems to be a source of some pride for her. The sleeping mats have no curtains around them – no privacy at all. I'm not up to that.

We go back into town to try to find a room. The GPS is working again and has several hotels listed. One by one we discover they are all booked out. Even the really expensive hotel has a wedding tonight and all the rooms are taken. We have no choice but to head back to the Pamir Lodge and see if we can pitch our tent in the garden.

On the way back we pass Mika. He turns around and tells us not to go back to the lodge. He explains it's not friendly at all. We have to make do with what is on offer and return to Pamir Lodge.

The only food I can find in the small market near the lodge is bread, yogurt and a couple of beers. It will do. I find the toilets and they are pretty rank but there are five of them, just as we've been told. The shower isn't the cleanest but the water is hot.

I leave Brian talking to Mika and Chris, a young Englishman who is riding to China. In the tent I have a meltdown. The roads, the heat, the lack of good food. It all mounts up. When Brian comes to bed he apologises for bringing me here. After the fabulous accommodation in Uzbekistan we are both surprised by the basic accommodation here. Tomorrow is another day.

•

There is fresh bread for breakfast and I have my tube of Vegemite. This cheers me up no end.

•

It's only a short ride today and the road isn't too bad considering what we've been through. Brian even manages to get the bike into top gear a couple of times! The scenery is beautiful. We're still paralleling the Afghanistan border and across the Panji River we can see into Tajikistan's neighbour. It's very desolate over there. At one stage we see a family group – the men leading a donkey carrying a woman, along a

The remains of a 2nd century fort

It's a rugged landscape

On the road back to Dushanbe

The narrow, winding road

narrow path. We can't work out where they have come from or where they are going.

We bump into the Aussies on the road again today. They are pushing on because they've heard there is a horse event in Murgab on the weekend and it's a good two-days' drive if they keep moving until dark. There's no way we want to ride such long distances on these roads.

•

There are more permit check points today. At one the soldier gives Brian a tin of Russian beef as a gift. Well, I presume it's beef because of the sketch of a cow with horns on the label.

At the guesthouse in Ishkashim we get a room in a back wing. We have to share a toilet with just one other room and there are two bathrooms inside the main house with clean showers. For just US$18 we get dinner and breakfast too. Everything is looking up. I'm even feeling hungry.

Brian offers the tin of meat to Varli, the guesthouse owner. He tells us we shouldn't eat this. It's army rations from a long forgotten war. He drops it in the bin.

Varli is collecting food and toiletries for the families who lost everything in the landslide. The tinned beef isn't going to them. We offer him the pencils Gio gave us for the kids in Mongolia. Brian and I agree this is a worthy cause. These families lost everything when their homes were washed away. Varli appreciates the offer and says the children will be thrilled.

•

Chris, whom we met last night in Khorug, arrives during the afternoon. He's a tall, gangly young Pom, standing head and shoulders above Brian. He has a wicked sense of humour and I'm really enjoying listening to the stories of his ride. He's heading to China and, in preparation for his trip, he's learnt a little of every language he'll need. Now, that's preparation!

At dinner he's ahead of me in the line for the food. I'm really looking forward to a decent meal. Chris lifts the lid on one of the pots and leans over for a close look.

'Ah, mystery meat stew,' he says as he puts the lid back on.

Thanks, Chris. There goes my appetite. Another night of just bread and fruit.

Brian: We're off to a good start today. The breakfast of eggs and fresh bread with homemade jam even tempts Shirl's appetite.

The sun is shining and Chris is happy for us all to ride together. Tonight we're going to camp somewhere on the far side of Layangar. He says he prefers a bit of company when he free camps and I know Shirl will feel safety in numbers. We have some tuna and noodles. It will be a meal fit for a king, served under the stars.

What I don't tell Shirl is that two Italian riders who came into the guesthouse last night told me that the road ahead of us is very difficult with plenty of sand, rocks and water. They advise me to take care. After breakfast we ride out, heading east along the river.

•

We can see into Afghanistan again today. There's a bit more activity, but not much. The odd small farm with buildings and fences made from mud. Water pumped from the river turns them into vibrant oases rather than dustbowls.

We stop at the remains of a 2nd Century BC fort. Made from mud there's not much left but I am surprised you can actually make out turrets on the outer wall. Chris hikes off to the top of the ruins. He's a lot fitter than us, and as Shirl points out, he's a lot younger. He's actually younger than Stephen and Gavan, my two sons!
Just because I can, I throw a rock into Afghanistan.

•

The road is getting worse. The sandy patches are getting bigger and deeper. Because the main road from China is cut by the landslide the trucks are down on this road and they are really chopping up the surface which probably isn't that great at the best of times.

I hit a deep, sandy patch and the bike just stops. I've hit a rock buried under the drift. The bike is standing upright, lodged into the sand. Even when we get off it's still standing there, on its own in about 15 centimetres of sand. It is funny, but trudging through the sand and pushing the bike is aggravating my torn calf muscle. Luckily Chris is behind us and helps me push it out. His bike is much lighter than ours and gets through the sand with ease.

Only a few kilometres along the road there's a traffic jam. This seems a little odd down here. We ride past the trucks and get to the source of the problem. A truck is bogged up to its axles in mud, leaning at a very precarious angle close to the edge of the road. People are trying to dig it out but it's going to take them forever.

I inch the bike past the truck, staying as far as possible from the steep drop off. There's not much room. One false move and we'll topple into the fast flowing river. Past the road hazard the line of trucks is growing. Drivers are squatting next to their trucks, patiently waiting to get on the road again.

We ride on and into another sandy bog but this time we don't just bog the bike, we drop it. It's a soft landing into about 30 centimetres of fine, white sand. I think I might have hit the sand a bit fast. The bike is so heavy it's fantastic to have Chris here to help pick it up.

No damage to bike or riders, just a slightly bruised ego!

Shirley: Certainly it is an easy fall. The only drama is the sand is so fine it gets into everything. I can feel it in my boots and my jacket pockets. This is one to tease Brian about!

We're not far from Layangar and our overnight stop. There should be fuel in the town but before we can get to it there's a fairly wide water crossing to get through. The road underneath is broken. Brian guns it through and my boots get a good wash.

There's an old petrol tank on the side of the road but no sign of anything that looks like it is still serving fuel. A group of local men sitting in the shade of a tree on the side of the road point back the way we came. The fuel is at Zong – on the other side of the water crossing. Back we go for another boot wash.

•

Brian: After the dust, dirt and sand this water crossing should settle some of the dust. Now the bike's air intake sits just above the right-hand cylinder and just below the tank. I know that I can cross water up to the cylinders without too much trouble.

There's some kids playing near the edge and they point to the best place to cross. Okay, gun it and let's see. It's all good until the last two metres. Suddenly the water is very deep, well over the cylinders, but there is no turning back. More power and we create a huge bow wave of water splashing over the top of the screen. Thankfully, it's only narrow and we make it out the other side without drowning the bike. The kids fall about laughing.

Shirley: Back on the other side of the water crossing there's a whitewashed building off the side of the road. We presume it's the fuel even though there isn't a sign. As soon as we pull up a man comes running from one of the houses. He unlocks the shed and reveals a tank of 92 RON, a collection of metal jugs and a funnel. It's pretty upmarket – the funnel has its own filter! It's back to basics when he overfills Chris' bike. He puts a piece of old hose in the tank and sucks on it to get the fuel flowing. Risky business.

As well as running the petrol station, he runs the local store and rushes off down the hill to open up so we can get a cold drink. He's been studying English and is proud to show off his skills, telling us he is building a guesthouse above the shop. He's a real go getter and will have the tourist trade sown up when it's all up and running.

Fuelled up and refreshed we head off back through the water crossing for the third time. On the other side, taking a break under some trees, we meet up with a group of Italian bikers coming the other way.

Their conversation is full of doom and gloom. They are trying to convince Brian and me to turn back, insistent that we won't make it through to the end of the M41. They say Chris will get through on his lighter bike and being one-up.

'The road is very bad. There is a 50-metre-wide river crossing with large rocks hidden in the water.'

It doesn't sound good at all. One of them shows Brian a video of the group manhandling their bikes across the river, one bike at a time. They even camped by the river hoping the water level would drop during the night. It didn't.

I'm not sure what to think. Brian is going to give it a try and I don't blame him. We've come this far.

As we ride out of town one of the Italians rides out with us. I presume he's going our way, but he's not. He's trying to convince us to turn around. He keeps gesturing and pointing back. When we keep going he shakes his head and turns back to his friends.

•

On the far side of the town the road starts to climb away from the river. It becomes a dog track more than a road. It's steep and sandy with large patches of big rocks across the width of the road. There's no

A local boy with his herd
Small world - we meet Albertino and discover we have mutual friends in Australia

riding around them. I can tell Brian is trying to manoeuvre our way through, avoiding the rocky patches and the sand as best he can. The sun is so bright it's hard to see where the packed sand ends and the soft sand begins.

It is impossible.

One minute we are going up a steep, tight left-hand corner. The next second we are lying on the track again. It happens so quickly there is no time to think about it.

Brian tries to hold the bike up with his bad leg, but the bike doesn't have any grip in the soft sand.

I fall hard and hit my head on some rocks.

I'm over it. I start to cry from shock and a little bit of pain. Brian keeps saying sorry – he's got nothing to be sorry about. This is a shit road and that is that.

He and Chris struggle to get the bike upright. With the bike settled Brian comes back to see if I'm alright. I tell him I can't go on. I look up at the road and know we'll drop it again and again. It's only a matter of time. We're too big and too heavy. I feel that I am letting Brian down but I just don't think I have it in me to keep on going up this hard road when we've been told it just gets worse.

The problem is the M41 is closed and all the trucks are coming along this road, breaking it up and making it even worse than it is normally. Brian agrees with me that we should turn back. He doesn't want to put me through any more. I love this man.

Brian: Shirl has fallen off from a fair height because of the width of the panniers and hit her head on a rock. She seems a bit dazed. I can't help her straight away because the bike is in the middle of the track. As I've come off I've re-torn my calf and it's bloody painful. I'm working against gravity to right the bike uphill. Stupid. I need to turn it around and use the slope.

Chris comes around the corner and the first thing he sees is Shirl sitting on the edge of the road. Farther around the bend he sees me, struggling with the bike. He dismounts and helps me move the bike just as a 4WD comes around the corner and just misses us. Shirl can't believe they didn't stop to help us.

When I get to her, she's crying and saying she can't go on.

I feel responsible. Sure I wanted to do this road, and I believe she did too but the elements, the incessant truck traffic and raging river we know is in front of us all seem too much right now.

When we do these trips it's for both of us. Shirl is okay. She's not hurt but has a bit of a headache. As we sit on the rocks I tell her we are a team. If we think it's getting too hard then okay, that's it, we go back. We've achieved our aim of getting down into the Pamir and the Afghan border. We are at the very end of that section and now heading up into the mountains, so going back means we'll miss maybe three or four hundred kilometres that's all.

Chris has to push on to meet the others he is travelling across China with. They're going to share the cost of the required guide, driver and car escorts which is really the only way independent travellers can get into China.

We say our farewells.

We are so thankful Chris was there to help us, a real traveller.

Thanks mate.

Shirley: We wish Chris good luck for the rest of his journey. Brian tells me he feels like an idiot and Chris must think he's incompetent. I doubt that – and if he does, so what. We never dreamt the road would be this bad.

I'm feeling a bit 'sprained'. My back is aching, my head is aching and I feel like I've hurt my hip. Nothing major, just nuisance level stuff.

Brian admits now that he's hurt his other leg hitting the bike when we fell and damaged his injured calf muscle even more when he put his leg down to try to stop the bike from falling.

We decide to push on back to Ishkashim. At least we know the guesthouse has pretty good food and a clean bed. It's only 3 o'clock. We should be there well before dark. At the water crossing Brian guns the bike and we get covered in water – for the fourth time.

The Italians are still in town and seem very glad that we've turned back. Even taking it slowly it would be hard on such a big bike two-up. Even without a lot of our luggage the bike is still heavy. The only way to take a lot of weight off it is for me to get off – and that's not an option. We've only come across one couple riding this road two-up. They were heading the other way a few days ago and admitted they'd had trouble,

The river races past our hotel, Kalaikhum

The President's propaganda posters

but it was easier coming down the bad roads than climbing up them.

I just wonder if we'd have done a bit better if Brian was 100 per cent. Maybe. Maybe not. We'll never know.

We are cautious riding through the sand on the way back. The patch that bogged us down is even bigger now. The wind has picked up and it's pushing more sand into the drifts across the road. I opt to get off and give Brian a better shot at getting through.

He does it easily but it's a long slow walk up the hill for me. I can't even take my helmet off because of the wind blowing the sand, making it a very strenuous walk. The heavy bike gear and boots don't help either.

We plod on and with every bump Brian groans – his legs are obviously giving him grief.

•

Back at the guesthouse Varli is surprised to see us but welcomes us back, offering us our old room. I'm a little taken aback that the beds haven't been changed!

We explain what's happened and Varli immediately offers to take Brian to the hospital. That won't be necessary. He just wants to rest.

I need a drink. I know there's a shop in town that sells whisky so I trudge up the hill, past the monument of Lenin's head and yet another poster of the Tajikistan President. The store is shut.

There's another market in town. Hopefully they will have some. The shopkeeper has vodka so I ask for her best. It has a bear on the label and it's Russian so it must be good. I don't know how much it costs and I don't care. I order a bottle of cola to go with it and wait for the bad news. Totting it up on her abacus (yes, she uses an abacus) she writes down the sum for me – 26 somoni. That's less than US$4.

The soup tonight is good. The vodka is better. Varli lights a fire and we sit out there for a while, mulling over our day. It could have been so much worse.

Brian: I need a rest but Ishkashim isn't the spot. I know there is a good hotel in Khorug. It was booked out when we came through a few days ago. Hopefully we can get a room tonight.

It's not a long ride and there's no surprises along the way. The mountains and the river are as beautiful as they were a couple of days ago and the road just the same.

The Hotel Lal has a delightful garden hidden behind a high stone wall. It's a long way from the sand and rocks of the road. We take a double room with private bathroom, cable TV and a small fridge for just US$65 a night.

Shirl didn't drink all of her vodka last night. It goes straight into the freezer. It is perfect as an icepack to heal my wounds from the outside and as a tipple to heal our wounds from the inside.

Sitting in the garden we bump into Bryn, a NZ biker I've been following on the Net. He's staying in one of the dorm rooms while he waits for his Afghanistan visa to come through. The little café attached to the hotel cooks up a brilliant pizza and some hot chips – comfort food. We get talking to a young German couple who've been hiking in the mountains for the past 15 days. They are eating their weight in comfort food, trying every restaurant in town.

•

We visit the tourist office to see if there is a road we can get to Kyrgyzstan without going back through Dushanbe. One border is closed to foreigners. The other is on the other side of the landslide. Apparently bicycles and hikers can get through by walking down to the river and going past the landslide by boat. That's not possible for a big bike like ours. The only way for us is to go back through Dushanbe.

•

Back at the hotel I get talking to a group of Swiss riders who are doing a motorcycle tour organised by Muz Too, a company owned by the Swiss but based in Osh, Kyrgyzstan. They are very sympathetic about our position. Their support car driver says it's a pity we didn't meet a few days ago. They could have taken Shirl and the luggage in their car. It would certainly have made life easier, but it was not to be.

I need some brake pads and hoped to ship them from Australia to Osh. The international courier company has told my mechanic Phil Marshall, back in Melbourne, that the only thing they will ship to any country whose mail goes through Russia are documents – certainly not motorcycle parts. I can understand that after the hassle we had getting a parcel out of Moscow. Unlucky for us, all mail to Kyrgyzstan, like Uzbekistan, goes through Russia. Maybe Muz Too could be the solution to my brake problem. I'll keep them in mind.

Lenin, Ishkashim

A casual looking President, Kalaikhum

Shirley: Things are looking up. Breakfast is a feast of omelette, pancakes, cheese and yoghurt and I devour it. Brian's leg is swollen and a very peculiar colour from his knee to his ankle, but he says he's on the mend.

We farewell the Swiss bikers on their journey and just hang out in the garden. It ends up being like old home week. Iain, the cyclist we met in Kalaikhum arrives. Another couple in the garden look familiar but I can't put my finger on where we've met. Alain and Linda are travelling around Central Asia using local buses and hire cars with drivers. It sounds like a pretty good way of seeing this beautiful region while leaving the stress of driving on the roads up to others.

Linda produces her iPad and it all falls into place. I remember her from the restaurant at *Lyab-i-Hauz* in Bukhara. They were sitting next to us and she was on Skype, showing whoever she was talking to the pool and the restaurant. It's a small world.

The conversation turns to the roads and our dramas. Iain suggests we take the paved road back to Dushanbe rather than the pass. Linda and Alain have just driven the road and say it is OK, mostly good pavement.

It's a plan. We're going to take the road of least resistance.

•

There is a concrete swimming pool on the edge of the river in Ishkashim. It is the place to get away from the heat. It is packed with people enjoying the water. It dawns on me that there are only boys and young men swimming. No girls. Thinking back to the swimming holes, irrigation channels and creeks throughout the Pamir there were no girls swimming there either.

Back at the hotel some of the bikes from the Swiss tour are in the parking area. One is damaged. One of the riders came off and is being evacuated home with a broken leg.

We were really lucky not to have suffered serious injuries.

•

We backtrack to Kalaikhum and try another guesthouse in the town. Dinner, bed and breakfast for US$20 seems to be the going rate. This place is certainly downmarket in comparison with the lovely Hotel Lal. The garden is a concrete pad overlooking the river. The toilet and shower are on this level. Our room is one level up. It has no door or bed. The owner assures us the bed will be there before it is time to go to sleep.

There's another cyclist staying here. Patrick is an incredibly fit 50-something who is on his way from his home in Switzerland to China. It seems to be the place to head to. Independent travel in China is difficult, so we are sticking to our plan to ride across Siberia.

This is a very strange guesthouse. The owner goes into the shower and after about 10 minutes he opens the door and whistles. His wife appears from the kitchen and scurries across to join him. They are in there together for about 20 minutes and then she comes out and goes back to preparing dinner. I am gobsmacked.

We both sleep fitfully. The glassless windows and a hole where the door should be don't offer privacy or soundproofing.

Tomorrow we'll hit the road for Dushanbe, taking the sealed road.

Brian: Hopefully today's ride will be a simple one.

The road is sealed – at first. On this good section of road taking us along the Afghan border, heading south before we turn north for Dushanbe, we pass a group of Russian bikers. They tell us the road is good and then bad and then very bad and then it is all clear sailing to the capital. We knew it couldn't be this good the whole way.

On the first gravel section Shirl tells me something hit her foot. Our tracker has fallen out of the tank bag. Luckily the bright orange device stands out on the road. It would have been a drama if we'd lost this. Every day it sends a message to our family at home, telling them where we are and that we are safe.

•

It seems like everyone thinks this is the best way to get to Dushanbe. The traffic is much heavier than over the pass. There are numerous small towns, with police checks, so the going is slow. Many of the drivers are keen to get a close look at us – so close it's dangerous. The trucks are spewing out black fumes. The air is so dirty you can feel it on your face, in your eyes and in your mouth.

I think I prefer the road less travelled than this nightmare of traffic congestion where drivers don't use indicators and most of the vehicles don't have brake lights. It is a test of man and machine.

•

Back in Dushanbe, the hotel's housekeeper gives me a big hug while we're checking in.

We go back to old faithful, Moscow Café for dinner and are greeted by the thumbs up from the waiters. The owner has hugs and kisses for both of us and turns on the fountain. We obviously made an impression last time we were here.

•

Shirl is not all that happy when I tell her I'd like to take the 'Tunnel of Fear' on our way out of town. I'm sure she thinks I'm crazy, but there is nothing like it anywhere else in the world.

Lucky for Shirl but unlucky for me the tunnel is still closed so we ride back over the mountains fighting the trucks, the potholes and the heat.

•

We have only one more night in Tajikistan, at a hotel near the border, before we cross into Kyrgyzstan.

Back into Russia through Kyrgyzstan and Kazakhstan

13 – 19 August 2015

Brian: Other travellers have told us that Kyrgyzstan is a dream in comparison to the other 'Stans' when it comes to bureaucracy. Rather than complicated paperwork and expensive fees, the visa for this country is just a stamp at the border and it's free.

Getting out of Tajikistan is a simple process. No forms to fill in. No searches.

We have a little wait at the Kyrgyzstan gate before a guard comes out, opens up the country and lets us in. We are ushered into an office to fill in the paperwork for the motorcycle. There is a fee involved – 500 som which is less than AUD$10. The only problem is we don't have any local currency yet. Shirl was planning on changing some money at the border and then going to an ATM when we get to Osh tonight.

The border guards aren't fazed at all. We don't have the cash. They don't take foreign currency so they just give us the form without having to pay the fee.

•

On the road we stop at the first town, Batken, so Shirl can get some money. There were no money changers at the border and she doesn't want to wait until we get to Osh.

While she sorts out the finances I sort out the ride to Osh. There are several areas in this part of Kyrgyzstan that are actually enclaves of Uzbekistan. I have to avoid these as we don't have a valid Uzbek visa, already using our single entry.

The bank won't change money and Shirl is directed to the market to seek out the black market money changers. From where I'm parked I see her deep in conversation with a local. She hasn't had to find the money changers, after all. One of them has come to her. He saw her wad of Tajik currency when she was in the bank and will change 1100 for 1000 som. It's the official rate.

•

I'm sure I'm on the right road. The road is in tip-top condition and the ride through the hills is the best we've had for days. My joy comes to an abrupt halt when we come to a border. While trying so hard to avoid Uzbekistan I've ridden right to the border of one of the enclaves.

The guards get their boss who demands to see our passports. I'm hoping we can talk our way through. The main road to Osh is just on the other side of this barbed wire fence. Surely this isn't going to be a problem. I'm not sure if it is a good sign or a bad sign when the officer and our passports disappear into his office.

It is a bad sign. There is no way the guards are going to let us through. This is Uzbekistan and only locals are permitted to pass – even with a valid Uzbek visa these enclaves are closed to foreigners. We have no choice but to turn back to Batken and find another way through.

It's a very confusing place, this part of Kyrgyzstan. The Uzbekistan enclaves are closely guarded to make sure no one without the proper paperwork wanders in there by mistake (like us).

•

We backtrack and put another town in the GPS. This time we are on the right road. We do go past another bit of Uzbekistan but this enclave is clearly marked and on a side road, easily avoided.

I am having a great ride. The road is good, gentle curves around green hillsides. There's virtually no traffic and no road hazards. I've missed this kind of riding.

•

Shirley: They might not thrive on paperwork but Kyrgyzstan loves its roadblocks. We are pulled up, yet again. I sometimes think they just want to look at the bike.

When one of the guards takes our passports into the office I get off the bike and fill in time by getting out our snack bag and having a jelly lolly we'd bought at a supermarket in Dushanbe. One of the guards

The Russia / Kazakhstan border

On the road to Semey, Kazakhstan

An Uzbekistan enclave in the heart of Kyrgyzstan

The men still wear the traditional headwear, Kyrgyzstan

comes up and puts out his hand, taking some lollies when I offer him the bag. With a cheeky smile, he opens the snack bag and rummages through what's left of our roadside snacks. I have a few wafer biscuits with vanilla cream left. I bought them in Russia and they're a particular favourite. I'm hoping I can replenish them when we cross the border. When he goes to help himself I voice my disapproval with a furrowed brow and a 'hey'. He smiles again, closes the bag and gives it back to me.

Our passports are returned and we're on our way. I don't give this stop another thought.

We haven't gone very far and another official walks out in front of the bike and motions for us to move off the road. We know the procedure. Brian gets the passports out and gives them to him. This time we don't get off the bike.

One of the police, or at least we think they are police, takes our passports. The guard, dressed in the same khaki uniform as our food thief, is gesturing that he is hungry. I am flummoxed. Brian can't work out what he's going on about.

Within minutes our passports and back and we're on the road. I get thinking about this strange stop. The man who took our passports didn't seem at all interested in us. We seemed to be an inconvenience. The other man's gestures – was he after food?

Suddenly it dawns on me. His mate must have radioed through and told him about our food bag. Maybe this second stop was a bit of a joke – a chance for him to get some of our lollies – and not a serious stop at all. That's the only thing we can think of. What an odd thing to do. Maybe the joke would have been funny if we all spoke the same language.

Brian: Finally, we get to Osh and hit yet another roadblock, this one right across the road from our hotel. I can see it, but the police manning the barricade don't want to let us through and I don't want to backtrack. After much pointing and pleading the police shift the barrier and let me ride through. I can't work out why the road is closed, but it's irrelevant now we are past.

Shirley: Our hotel is the Osh-Nuru, one of the remnants of the city's

Soviet past. It's a concrete monolith with a small tourist office in the foyer offering tours of Russia and flights on Aeroflot, and a swimming pool in the front yard. The Bondi to Baltic boys had recommended another hotel but it was booked out, so this will have to do.

While the outside of the hotel doesn't look as though it has changed much, our room is pretty stylish. It is actually a suite with a small lounge room with a television and fridge. The bedroom has a balcony overlooking the pool that seems to be 'the' place to be on this hot afternoon. It is packed with locals who pay a small fee for permission to swim. I won't be joining them. My bathers were one of the items sent home from Germany.

The first thing I do is check out the TV for an English language news service. I reckon Brian is quietly pleased that there's no English TV at all. He's quite enjoying being away from TV, while I miss it.

Some of the staff speak a little English and the restaurant has an English language menu. A bowl of pasta is the simplest thing I can find listed. I haven't had much of an appetite for a couple of weeks. I'm nearly out of Gastro-Stop so I'd better try to find a chemist tomorrow. It has been nearly impossible to avoid eating foods washed in the water and that's probably has been upsetting my apple cart.

Brian: I leave Shirl washing the bike gear, making the most of the balcony to get it dry, and head to Muz Too. The bike needs some TLC and the Swiss-owned business is just the place. I know they have a mechanic who speaks English and you can use their tools to work on your own bike for a small fee.

I ride through the back streets of Osh with the GPS directing me down little narrow dirt streets and lanes. Just as I think I'm lost, I spy a two-storey house with a small garage and a bike parked out the front. I'm waved through into a big open courtyard in front of an open, barnlike shed with heaps of bikes parked, many with foreign registrations. This is Muz Too.

There's a young hippie couple loading huge backpacks onto a sagging KLR 650 Kawasaki and a mechanic pulling apart a gearbox. I am welcome to use any of the facilities for a donation of the equivalent of US$20 and the price of any parts I want, not that they have much for BMWs. They hire out robust old Yamaha 650cc singles and have

The scenery is breathtaking on the road from Osh to Toktogul, Kyrgyzstan

A natural road hazard, Kyrgyzstan

Magnificent scenery on the road from Osh to Toktogul, Kyrgyzstan

enough bits and pieces lying around to build three bikes, I reckon.

I find a clear spot, pull out the air cleaner, adjust the valves and generally wash the bike to check things. All seems good except the rear brake pads are very thin and, stupidly, I don't have a spare set. The owner delves into the shipping container where they store all their spare parts and comes back with a box of brake pads. Searching through I'm lucky enough to find a set that will fit, even though they are not made for a BMW. It's an easy repair. A morning well spent.

Back at the hotel I find Shirl luxuriating on the coach, surrounded by our clean washing. Another much-needed task completed successfully.

Shirley: With the washing done, I walk the streets trying to find the chemist the hotel staff told me exists but I can't find it. There's not a lot to see in this part of Osh, just a couple of small grocery shops and restaurants that are closed. The road across from the hotel is still barricaded off, for no apparent reason.

A lack of good food and the heat are taking their toll on me. Every day is a chore. I don't feel sick but I don't feel well. I try not to harp on it because Brian has got enough on his plate just taking care of the bike and dealing with the roads. Given half a chance, I'd love to go home. Brian, quite rightly, is keen to finish the ride that we started. We're going to Vladivostok or bust.

•

We're heading north to Toktogul, hopefully without bumping into Uzbekistan. It doesn't take long to get out of town and rather than the road turning into a nightmare it is good. It's sealed, smooth and takes us through the most amazing mountains. Brian is really enjoying himself. There are a few crazy drivers around, but not too many. This ride is one of the best we've had for days, weeks even. And it's not too hot. Woo hoo!

The green hills are dotted with horses grazing alongside yurts built by the nomadic people who come to these pastures during spring and summer. Tiny streams glisten in the sun.

This is the kind of day we both love.

•

Damien recommended a guesthouse in Toktogul. I've contacted the owner over the Internet so he should be expecting us. As usual, finding the address is a little complicated.

Brian pulls up on the side of the road in the town to check the map and see if we can find the street. Two boys in their early teens come over to see if they can help. They speak perfect English and are quite pleased when we compliment them on their language skills.

They're giving Brian directions to the guesthouse when I hear the squeal of brakes behind us. One of the young men's eyes widen as big as saucers. He grabs his friend and lets out a scream. Something has gone horribly wrong behind us.

In a second the drama passes and the boys tell us a driver, trying to avoid an old man on a bicycle, didn't see us until he was about to hit us! That was a close call.

Wouldn't it be ironic to have a major accident while stationary on a good road, rather than motoring along on one of the shocking roads we've been on!

•

At the guesthouse the boss is away and the young lady who is in charge doesn't speak any English and wasn't expecting us. One of the other guests speaks a little Russian and explains we want a bed and dinner. There's room for us, outside another guest room. Andrew, a young Englishman who is about to embark on a hiking holiday through the mountains, doesn't mind us being right outside his door.

I go up the street to get Brian a couple of beers. They have Baltika, a Russian beer that comes in various strengths. Brian has been enjoying the Baltika 7 but the local shop has only Baltika 11. It's nearly as strong as wine. Brian and Andrew enjoy the cold beers a little more than usual!

Dinner is a spicy soup with some of Chris' mystery meat floating in it. The salad has been prepared in the water over the drain, so I give it a miss. What I can't resist is the sweet jam made from some local berries. It is delicious.

Breakfast is congealed fried eggs that were probably cooked hours ago. The honey to sweeten the tea has become home to a family of flies, making it less than appetising.

I break out the Vegemite and some biscuits that are in our emergency food supply. Saved again by this Australian favourite.

A yurt camp on the road to Bishkek, Kyrgyzstan

Horses wandering across the road, Kyrgyzstan

A yurt camp on the road to Bishkek, Kyrgyzstan

Green pastures and snow-capped mountains, Kyrgyzstan

Brian: We get some fuel and head back on the road to Bishkek. I can't believe the ride is even better than yesterday. The climb up to the 3184-metre Ala-Bel Pass is gentle, taking us through more green fields and past more nomad yurt camps.

Horses, many with foals, sheep and lambs, goats and kids are all grazing on the lush pastures.

When we get to the top there is another gentle road down into the meadows. This is so beautiful. We can't believe the scenery, the weather and the condition of the road!

The next pass, Töö-Ashun is more than 3500 metres and even more dramatic. The mountains that soar around us are spectacular. The meadows give way to rivers flowing through the rocky outcrops.

The beauty all ends too soon as we hit the outskirts of Bishkek – just another big city. Even though it's Sunday the traffic is hectic. There seem to be street markets around every corner. No one bothers to look, they just walk out across the road. Cars pull up to pick up passengers whether there is room for the traffic to get past or not. This is a strain on my nerves and my legs are aching, more and more, every time I have to put my feet down. Obviously my injuries aren't healed yet.

Shirley: This time the hotel recommended by the Bondi to Baltic boys has rooms and is perfect. The Asia Mountain 1 hotel has a beautiful, lush garden around a sparkling swimming pool. Rather than braving the traffic to go sightseeing, we head to the pool to swim and rest. Well, Brian swims. I just put my feel in the water, cursing the fact I sent my bathers home from Germany.

There's *Plov* on the menu for dinner, the Central Asian comfort food.

Clean sheets, a comfy bed, a pretty good meal. Bliss.

•

We're heading back into the unknown. We have a border to cross, back into Kazakhstan and then north to Russia. Overnight a message has come through from Damien reminding us that we are heading back into the land of the really bad roads. More's the pity. The roads in Kyrgyzstan have been terrific.

•

The border crossing isn't far from the city and it's pretty simple. Leaving the country, they don't even mention the fact we don't have any paperwork for the importation of the bike.

On the Kazak side there's plenty of pushing and shoving in the immigration queue. There's no problem with our double-entry visas, once we battle our way through the pushy locals.

The motorcycle paperwork is done quickly and everything is going swimmingly until we are directed to 'Rapid Scan'. It is a tin shed with massive double doors and a queue of six cars waiting outside. The doors creak open and an official waves Brian in and indicates that I should wait. All I can hear are dogs barking when the doors close again behind Brian.

In a couple of minutes, the doors creak open again and I'm beckoned in. It seems they didn't want to see the pillion until they discovered she has all the paperwork.

Inside there's the cutest little black dog barking at the bike. He's not indicating we are carrying any contraband. He just doesn't like bikes.

In the corner of the shed a car is sitting on jacks. Its four wheels are off and the four doors and boot are open. It's surrounded by a few boxes and a very unhappy man who is not enjoying the thorough going-over his car is getting. Hopefully they are not going to do that to us.

The first bag they want opened is mine. Why is it always mine – the hardest one to close again because of all the stuff I am carrying? The officials lose interest very quickly when they find just women's clothing inside. We can go.

At the exit the officials are sitting under an awning, their guns propped up against the wall. They order us to go back towards the gate to Kyrgyzstan. This isn't right. We go back to the exit and Brian growls that we've been through Rapid Scan and should be heading to Kazakhstan. One of the men drags himself off his seat and checks the paperwork. We're right to go. If only he'd got off his fat arse in the first place.

I remember our motto and smile at him. Rule number one – always smile at the man with the AK47. Rule number two – always smile at the man who has the stamp to get you into the country.

As the gate closes behind us the money changers appear. We get some more Kazakhstan currency and, this time, make sure we get the insurance we need.

An abandoned factory, Kazakhstan

Horses graze in the summer pastures, Kyrgyzstan

They love their statues in this part of the world

Brian: Shirl hasn't got the market cornered when it comes to homesickness. I'm missing my boys and our five grandchildren. Today is one of those days when the littlest things annoy me. Our Almaty hotel bill is stacked with a 20 percent tax and 10 percent service fee. It was clean and a little luxurious but these extras make it a very expensive night.

I'm really looking forward to getting back into Russia. We've arranged to meet our good friends Ken and Carol Duval in Barnaul in a few days. It can't come soon enough.

We first met these Queenslanders when we got back from our first trip in 2004 and were asked to speak at a Horizons Unlimited travellers' meeting. Since then they've been on the road, riding around the world at a very leisurely pace. We spent time together in Canada and Alaska back in 2012. It is going to be fantastic to be with them again. There is something special about meeting up with fellow Aussies on the road.

•

It's a long ride from Almaty to Semey, the next major centre on the road to the Russian border, and I know we won't make it one day, even if the roads are good, which we know they won't be. We are back in Kazakhstan, after all. I have no idea if there will be a hotel or guesthouse along the way. I warn Shirl, if worst comes to worst we'll camp somewhere along the way. We still have our tuna and noodles that we were going to use in Tajikistan.

The road is very much as we expected. It goes from OK to potholes, to big potholes and then back to OK. The going is slow.

It's getting towards 4pm and I am getting tired. This is when mistakes can happen, when a lapse in concentration can end in disaster.

I look for hotels in the GPS but the nearest ones are more than 100 kilometres away and in the wrong direction. There is no way I'm going away from the Russian border, particularly on these roads.

I push on and check again. This time I find a bed about 60 kilometres away on the road to Semey in a tiny dot on the map – Aqtoghay. It's a two-storey building with no signage to indicate it's a hotel, but that means nothing. I ride into a parking area at the back of the building and a woman appears at the door. She takes Shirl inside.

It is a hotel. They have a room with twin beds near the shower and toilet area. There's a fridge filled with cold drinks in the foyer, so there is no discussion. We take it. The temperature got up to near 40°C again today and that is way too hot in all our motorcycle gear.

Shirley: A cold drink and a cold shower and then we take a walk through town. The busiest spot is the bus station. I'm not sure where all these people have come from or where they are going. There's an old factory across the road that seems to be abandoned. Farther down the street, behind a high wall, there's an empty building that once could have been an accommodation complex – maybe for the factory workers. Sticking up above the wall is a statue of Lenin. He's no longer the town's centrepiece, just a symbol of the past.

There's a mosque in town, with crimson and golden dome and minaret. The fading light adds to its beauty. This town must have been a bustling place once, but today there's not much here. When the bus leaves the streets are deserted. There's no café so we dine on the snacks we've been carrying in our panniers.

•

We've booked a hotel in Semey for our last night in Kazakhstan. It's another hot day, with the temperature already in the high 30s before lunchtime. We are riding through broad plains of dry paddocks and the occasional field of wheat. It's such a contrast to the fertile green hills of Kyrgyzstan.

We are about 150 kilometres from our destination when the road turns into a gravel pit. It's not just a gravel road. It is gravel several centimetres thick. It's hard going, literally ploughing through the thick layer of stones. Brian has strict instructions for me. 'Shut up and sit still.'

The stretch lasts for about eight kilometres and then turns into one of the best pieces of sealed road we've had all trip. These roads just do my head in!

Brian: Shirl worries when the road deteriorates. I understand that, but having her voicing her fears in my ears disrupts the concentration I need to get us through. She can talk all she likes when the road is good…and she does!

Semey is just an overnight stop for us. It is a town with a horrible past. The Soviet masters used an area around the town as a nuclear test

The road takes us through the mountain passes, Kyrgyzstan

site. For four decades, from the late 1940s, the Soviets conducted 456 nuclear tests here. They didn't tell the people living in the area about the tests. Today the community has major health problems, including high rates of cancer and birth defects.

The town is also home to a cemetery for Lenin busts and statues. I know Shirl would love to find this unique collection but I am tired. It's been a long couple of days, riding more than 600 kilometres each day, in extreme heat.

Our plan is to cross back into Russia tomorrow and head straight to Barnaul to meet Ken and Carol.

Western Siberia
Barnaul to Ulan Ude

20 August – 1 September

Shirley: We've booked the hotel in Barnaul recommended by Ken and Carol. Even on Booking.com there's a review saying it's good for overland travellers who need somewhere comfortable to rest up after travelling through Central Asia. That's us.

Each apartment has a kitchen so we can cook our own meals for a change. We certainly get sick of eating out when we are travelling, but before I can start planning our menu we need to get back into Russia.

•

We get on the road early and travel the 180 kilometres to the border by 10.30am. We prefer to get to a border early, before the guards get tired and grumpy.

Leaving Kazakhstan is pretty simple. We ride the bike to a shed at the back of the border where officials ask if we are carrying guns or narcotics and then give a laugh. They do a cursory check of the bags and then direct us to Immigration. Brian can ride around, but I'm told to walk. A quick stamp and we're on our way into no man's land and the Russian border.

There's a queue outside the gate. We don't panic. It was the same in Finland. The Russians only let a certain number of vehicles into the border area at any one time. We are the last one through when the gate is opened. On the Russian side everyone gets out of their cars and walks into an office. We follow suit. Inside there are officials processing all of the arrivals, on computer. We don't have to fill in any forms. The officials print the paperwork we need in Russian and just show us where to sign. It's a very simple process.

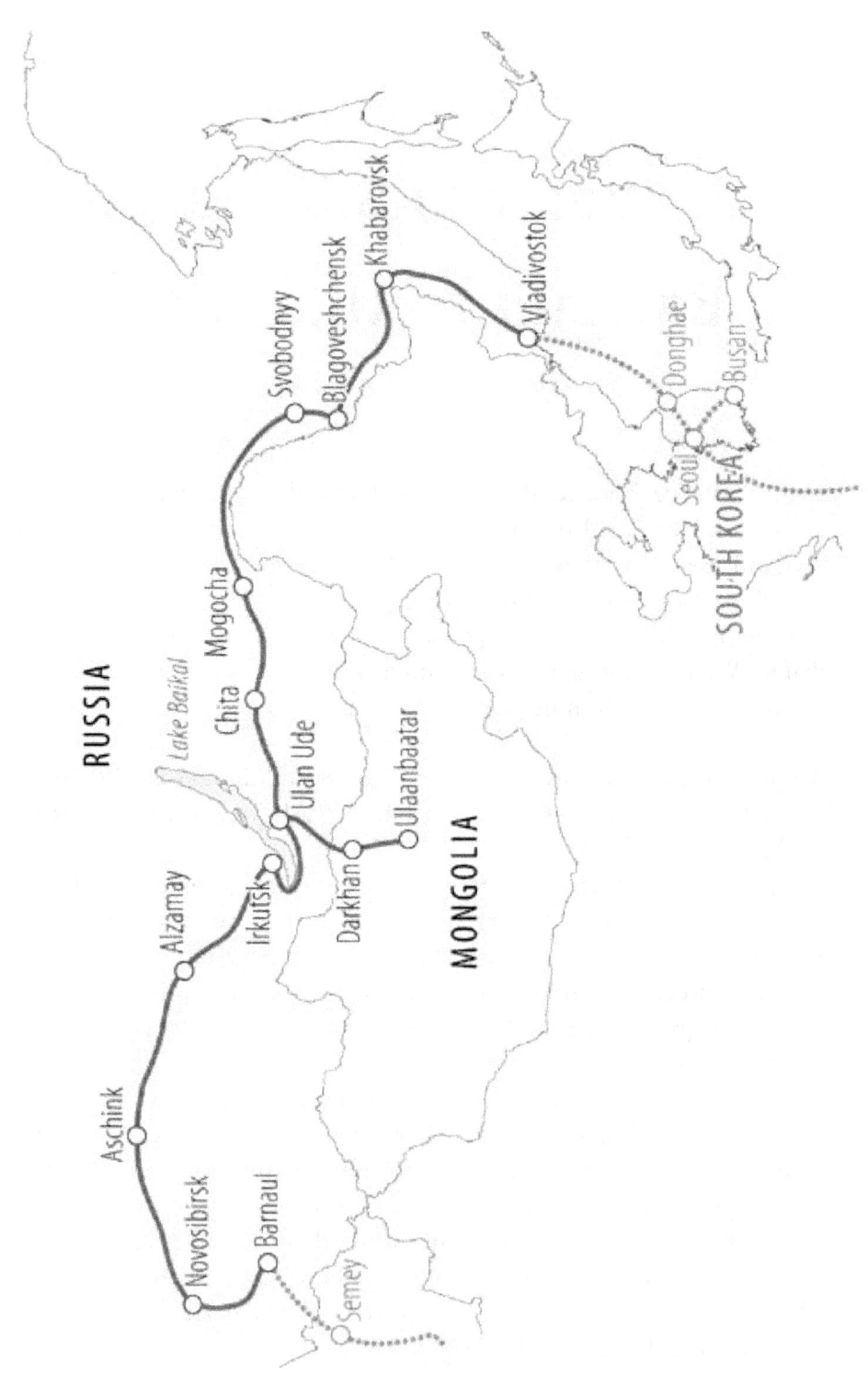

Outside, a young customs officer asks Brian to open my pannier. Why is it always my pannier? He shows no real interest in my bag or the tank bag. In less than two hours we are back in Russia and on the road to Barnaul.

•

The GPS takes us straight to the hotel, a nondescript brick building. There's no signage but we know it is the right place. There are a couple of overlander motorcycles parked out the front, but not Ken and Carol's old BMW R80GS.

The manager of the hotel, Paul, speaks English and explains Ken's gone to get his bike serviced, as he shows us our rooms. They are huge – a living room with a comfy couch and TV, kitchenette with full-sized fridge, massive king-sized bed and modern shower. This is fantastic. Sorry, Brian. They have an English language news channel so I can catch up with what's happening in the world.

But before I do that I head to the market to get a few supplies. In my haste to get there I leave the phrasebook and *Picture Talk* in the room. I'm not walking back to get it. I'll just muddle through.

It's only a small market but it sells all the essentials – groceries, bread, cheese, wine, vodka and Brian's favourite Baltika 7 beer. I load up and head to the counter where I get a lecture from one of the women behind the counter. I work out that it is really two shops in the one room and I have to buy the cheese, bread and milk from one counter and the rest from another. I give the women a smile and that 'I'm sorry, I'm a foreigner' look and they smile back. I'm sure I'm not the first confused by this.

Brian: I hear Ken's bike pull up. Shirl and I are both really looking forward to spending time with these veteran travellers. It's hugs and kisses all round.

I'm shocked by how Ken looks. He's a few years older than us, in his mid-60s. When we first met him in 2004 he'd just had a hip replacement. In 2012 his hips were working perfectly. Now he's slightly stooped and walking with a bit of a limp. It looks like he needs more work done on his joints.

While he might be a bit slower physically he's still a livewire, full of stories and advice. Carol is obviously thriving. She looks brilliant.

Shirl is looking forward to hanging out with Carol. She misses female company when we are on the road.

The Duvals cook good old-fashioned spaghetti bolognaise for dinner tonight. We eat in our apartment. The food is terrific; the beers are cold but the best thing is the friendship and the conversation.

Ken and Carol have spent years on the road and they are incredibly generous with their experiences and information they've gleaned along the way.

They have just arrived in Barnaul after riding from Mongolia via the dirt roads and river crossings. They admit it was hard going. At least once, when the going got too tough, they were forced to turn back to find another road. I'm glad we've decided to go into Mongolia from Ulan Ude. It's late August already and winter will arrive with a vengeance in Siberia and Mongolia soon. We need to make sure we're through to Vladivostok before that happens.

Shirley: Aussies love Vegemite. I always take it when we travel. It's my comfort food. Ken and Carol used the last of their supply a few weeks ago. I've been using mine sparingly so I can share the last of it with them. I am their favourite person when I produce the familiar yellow tube.

There are so many conversations to be had but we need sustenance, so we drag ourselves away from the apartment to replenish supplies. The trip to the supermarket is far from a chore. Our presence attracts a fair bit of attention, even while we are getting off the bikes.

We order some chicken pieces and Carol is very impressed that I know the Russian numbers. She is easily impressed. A little girl, who is probably about four, is watching our every move. Her mother speaks to her and the one word we understand is 'hello'. Encouraged by her mother the little girl, follows us around saying 'Hello, Hello' over and over again. She is delightful and even the reserved Russians, who are usually so hard to get to smile, are beaming at her antics.

The little one is a real ice-breaker. The woman in the bakery section gives us the freshest bread right out of the oven rather than the loaves on the shelf. Another young woman is a little shy, so she asks her husband to speak to us. They are very impressed when they find out we are from Australia.

A mural, Barnaul

With Lenin, Barnaul

Brian tries a new bike, Bikers' Bar, Barnaul

With the Russian bikers at the Bikers' Bar, Barnaul (Irina – far right)

Iron Riders Motorcycle colours, Biker's Bar   Interesting bar stool, Bikers' Bar

Our little girl friend comes out of the store with her mother while we are loading our goodies into the panniers. She has a new word, 'Goodbye', and she says it a hundred times until she's bundled into the car.

•

Walking along the corridors of the hotel we spot a familiar curly haired Kiwi sitting under the wireless router working on his emails. We last saw Bryn in Khorug in Tajikistan when he was waiting for his Afghanistan visa. He arrived in town last night with a Spaniard and an Israeli. It's a small world.

Bryn did get into Afghanistan but about 100 kilometres down the road he was turned back by the officials. Now he's on his way to Mongolia.

•

I love spending time with Carol. It's good to talk through some of the problems we have on the road, from a female perspective. The bike being too heavy is always the major issue when travelling two-up. We've sent home all manner of stuff – excess clothes, souvenirs, spare parts, camping gear we are unlikely to use – and still the bike is heavy.

'The only way to get any real weight off the bike is to remove the pillion passenger,' Carol says with a laugh.

It is funny, but true. Carol's actually offered to travel by bus and meet Ken at night to lighten the load. I haven't gone that far. A heavy bike is just the reality we all have to deal with.

The hard ride through Tajikistan, the heat and the bad roads take their toll and it is good to have a whinge with a woman who understands. I need a home base and I'm missing ours right now. I know life will improve soon. It only takes a couple of good rides, some interesting cities and I'm thriving on our life again.

•

Bar 13 is clearly the place to be in Barnaul. There is a queue outside but we get straight in and are seated at a big table in the back corner. There seems to be special treatment for visitors on one hand, but keep us out of the way on the other. There is no argument from us. The house speciality is fajita, a Mexican favourite. While in Barnaul do as the locals do…fajita all round. Bryn is with his new travelling companions – Elad and Ricardo, who looks very familiar to us.

Eventually we work it out. We met Ricardo in Atyrau on our first night in Kazakhstan. He ended up sharing a room with Damien that night. The day we arrived in Beyneu he was on his way to the Aral Sea in Kazakhstan. He hit a goat that day and ended up in a local hospital with broken ribs. We have been so lucky. I don't think I'd like to spend time in a hospital in this part of the world.

As we are leaving the family sitting at the next table ask where we are all from. Mum, dad and the two girls all speak perfect English. I hope we haven't been too outrageous during dinner. We need to be careful. You never know who can be listening.

Brian: The hotel has organised a city tour for us, with our own van, guide and interpreter – Irina. She is a very glamorous young woman who was a gymnast and still looks fit enough to compete. Her English is brilliant.

•

The Great Patriotic War deeply affected Russians right across the country, even here, so far from the front line. Thousands of Barnaul men died on the battlefields and the women of the city worked in the tank factory. Elad is keen to see the tank factory. He was a tank commander in the Israeli army and knows about the machines that were churned out here. The factory now makes more mundane machines so he has to make do with the tank that's across the road from the war memorial.

A poignant statue of a soldier saying goodbye to his mother is the centrepiece of the memorial. It is a moving image of the heartbreak of war.

Walking across the square Shirl is deep in conversation with Irina.

Shirley: Because of my childhood visit to the Soviet Union I am intrigued by the number of statues of Vladimir Lenin that have survived the fall of communism. It seems the people are happy to have this reminder of their communist past.

Irina is telling me that her favourite Lenin statue once stood quite close to this square but it was destroyed. One remains and we'll see that later in the tour.

I ask her what is was like here when communism came to an end.

'My grandparents lived in a village outside of the town and I

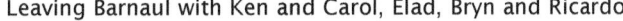
With Elad, Bryn, Ricardo, Ken and Carol at the tank memorial, Barnaul

Leaving Barnaul with Ken and Carol, Elad, Bryn and Ricardo

Brian and Ken

Lenin, Novosibirsk

The Novosibirsk Opera Theatre – bigger than the Bolshoi

remember visiting them and being shocked to see children in ragged clothes, begging on the streets. They were our children and they were starving.'

She explains that overnight the government-run factories closed. Thousands of people lost their jobs, people who were looked after by the government were left without support. 'There was no transition. Everything ended abruptly.

'It might have been OK for Moscow, but not here, in the country.'

It is food for thought. In the West we saw the jubilation of the Berlin Wall being pulled down, brick by brick, and celebrations on the streets of other communist cities. Irina doesn't say she yearns the days of communism but she doesn't say life in Russia is better today.

•

Our last stop of the day is the remaining Lenin statue. I'm getting quite a collection of photos of Lenin across Russia. The only place I didn't find one was Moscow, where he still lies in his mausoleum.

Brian: We are all starving so we decide to head out to the Biker Bar we've heard about for a late lunch. Irina asks if she can join us. Of course!

The bar is easy to find. The oversized bike out the front is better than any neon sign. It's mid-afternoon but there are half a dozen locals out the front having a smoke. They greet us with the usual Russian reservation, not overly friendly but not unfriendly.

Inside the bar is dark and dingy. Bikes are hanging from the ceiling and the walls, bike parts have been fashioned into tables and chairs. The bikers follow us in and ask us to join them. Thank goodness for Irina. She works hard all afternoon interpreting for all of us.

The locals have hangovers you can photograph and are working on another one. There isn't a bike in sight. Drivers are not permitted to have any alcohol in their bloodstream and the bikers seem happy to obey the law. They share their food with us – a barbecue platter with sausages and piles of chips – good Australian-style hangover cure food.

One of them is drinking a cold soup that he says is the perfect Russian hangover cure. It looks pretty disgusting. I don't think it would catch on in Australia.

They present each of us with a beer mug and a special badge they had struck to mark the 70th anniversary of the end of the Great Patriotic War. This is a wonderful gesture of friendship. We have to sneak some money to the barmaid when our hosts aren't looking, to pay for our share of the food and our beers.

As the afternoon goes on, one of the locals gets to the crying drunk stage. Irina tells us he has marriage problems and is missing his young daughter. He drapes his arm around Elad's shoulder and shares his sad tale with him even though the friendly Israeli can't understand a word of it.

When it comes time to leave he embraces us all, constantly weeping.

We get into Irina's car and are about to drive off when he yanks open the passenger door, leans across Shirl and says something to Irina. She politely declines what she tells us was an offer to come back to the bar when she drops us off.

Shirl jokes with her that if she was interested in a husband this could be the place for her to look!

•

Ken found a great little place that sells good oils and was servicing his bike there when we arrived. While Big Red is running fine, a bit of TLC for the next leg of our journey wouldn't go astray. Ken and I ride off for some 'man time' and leave the girls to whatever girls do when we're not around. Ken takes me into the shop to buy the oil from a gorgeous young woman – what the hell is she doing selling oils! With a smile she directs us around the back where there is a very clean workshop and two mechanics working on a pimped-up little car. As soon as they see us they drop everything. With sign language and rudimentary language, I tell them I can change the oils and have my own tools. They give me a pan for the old oils and sit back, intrigued by where I keep the tools, hidden under the bike's seat. Over a few laughs they watch me strip the bike down and change the engine and gearbox oils, then clean out the air cleaner. I'm sure they should have closed down some time ago but these friendly guys and the glamour puss stayed open just for us.

Shirley: There are plenty of drawbacks riding two-up. We can't carry too much luggage and the bike is heavy, but travelling together has

Traditional house, Irkutsk

Lenin, Irkutsk

Lenin beckons, Irkutsk

Traditional houses, Irkutsk

more advantages. It's clear to me that we are very lucky to be doing this trip together. Elad is missing his family. His girlfriend travelled with him for a while, but had to return to Israel. Ricardo's relationship has broken down while he has been away. It's tough for the boys.

•

It's time to get moving. We need to head east and Ken and Carol are on their way to Moscow, but there is the opportunity to spend one more night together in Novosibirsk, the capital of Siberia. On the way we stop at a service station and Carol is gobsmacked to find a clean toilet inside the building and a café serving hot drinks and sandwiches. She's used to the filthy hole-in-the-ground toilets in Siberia and Mongolia. I guess that's something for me to look forward to.

•

The convention centre is offering the best deal for bed and breakfast and a great location, right across the road from the stupendous Trans-Siberian railway station. Novosibirsk is famous for its opera house, the largest in Russia, even bigger than the Bolshoi Theatre in Moscow.

Back in 1962 my family met the lead tenor with the Novosibirsk Light Opera Company, Yuri. I often wonder what happened to this wonderfully generous and friendly man who took great joy in showing us around Moscow and Leningrad. I remember seeing the operetta he was performing in, The Rose of Montmartre, and visiting the Hermitage palace in Leningrad with him. One day he took me to the theatre and Mum and Dad told me they watched us walking, hand in hand, across Gorky Square with me chatting away. I didn't speak Russian and Yuri didn't speak English, but we managed to communicate. Mum always used to say she didn't know who was going to cry first when we said goodbye to Yuri, me or him. My heart broke saying farewell to him. It's funny, the things you remember, 53 years on.

We don't see the Opera Theatre at its best, covered as it is in scaffolding. Right nearby is another formidable statue of my mate Lenin, surrounded by larger-than-life statues of heroes of the Great Patriotic War.

For our last meal together, the Duvals and the Rixs choose the steak and sushi restaurant in the hotel. No Chicken Kiev or Beef Stroganoff – just delicious, fresh, Western food washed down with a little whisky.

I'll miss Ken and Carol's sage advice and the friendly banter of friends who have something very basic in common – the love of life and the joy of travel.

Brian: Saying goodbye always takes longer than expected so we hit the road for Achinsk too late. We're heading to Irkutsk, near the enormous Lake Baikal. It's a long ride and I've planned three 600 kilometre rides to get us there, so an early start today would have been helpful.

The road is nothing out of the ordinary – good sometimes, bad sometimes with some stretches of roadworks thrown in.

The way Russians do roadwork makes for an interesting ride. They scrape the surface of 10, 20 or even more kilometres of road surface and then dig it up. They top it with a 20 centimetre layer of rocks as big as cricket balls but don't use steamrollers to break the rocks down to gravel. That job is left up to the trucks. For us it's like trying to plough our way through the rocks. It's difficult riding and Shirl gets stressed, but with some concentration we get through.

•

We stop for fuel and there are no indoor toilets here. I check out the hole in the ground and tell Shirl not to bother. I'll find somewhere on the side of the road for her. Drop toilets are quite common in outback Australia but here they are disgusting. There's excrement all around the hole in the ground. I won't go any further. Let's just say even I find it appalling.

A group of women arrive while Shirl and I are having a drink. One goes in and comes out holding a hanky over her face, wiping shit off her shoes. Another refuses to go in.

I find a track off the road for Shirl. At the end we find a clapped-out little car with the 'Team Give us a Push' banner emblazoned on it. It's obviously taking part in yet another Mongolia rally. When they drive out they don't acknowledge us, which is a bit odd. I wonder what they were doing. With them gone she can duck behind some bushes. It's much cleaner than the toilet back at the service station.

We spend the night at the Bon Voyage, a new two-storey motel right on the highway. The room is cosy, they have Internet and a café where, with the help of *Picture Talk*, we get a pretty good meal.

•

Dirty drop toilets, lunch consisting of potato crisps, Coke and chocolate bars and seemingly never-ending stretches of roadworks make up the

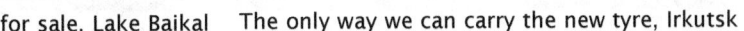

Lake Baikal emerges from the smoke

Smoked fish for sale, Lake Baikal   The only way we can carry the new tyre, Irkutsk

The USSR Pub on the banks of Lake Baikal

Lake Baikal

next two days on the road to Lake Baikal.

To break the journey, we pull in at a stop at a truck stop. Shirl sorts out the room and comes out with a huge grin. It's the first time she's had to tell the receptionist for how many hours we want the room The girl was surprised that we want it for the entire night. I guess truckies just spend a couple of hours showering, resting and then driving on.

The room is pretty good, it's certainly clean and the shower is hot. The café sells stews, dumplings and potatoes – good filling food. They must get some foreigners because they have an English menu.

•

The closer we get to Lake Baikal the more smoke there is in the air. A petrol station guard explains there are fires on the far side of the lake. They must be enormous for the smoke to be spreading this far. We are still more than 100 kilometres from Irkutsk and the lake.

Shirley: After three long days on the road we're both looking forward to some time off the bike, exploring the city of Irkutsk. There is a walking tour marked out on the town map that gives us the perfect route to take to see the best of this city in Eastern Siberia.

Unlike so many cities, Irkutsk hasn't bothered to change the names of the streets from the Soviet era. We walk down Karl Marx Street to Lenin Street and on to Lenin Plaza where there is, you guessed it, a bust of Lenin carved out of a massive piece of stone.

The streets are lined with traditional wooden buildings with their shuttered windows and carved doors. Some seem to be falling into disrepair, leaning at very odd angles with rot setting in. Other are beautifully restored, giving an insight into how stunning this city would have been in the 19th Century.

Hidden in the basement of one of these old buildings is the best burger restaurant we've found in more than four months on the road. We miss it completely on our first walk along the street. We're about to give up and head to a shopping centre for something to eat when we spot the sign for the Grill Restaurant. It makes burgers to order, with special combinations of homemade sauces, bacon, cheese and salads. The beer is icy cold and the local cranberry juice delicious – a much better meal than Pringles chips and Coke.

Continuing our walk through the city we pass the circus where they still have performing bears – a sign of the location. We end up at the river where a bride and groom and all their guests are having their photos taken at an ornate gateway on the banks of the river.

Back at the hotel the peace and quiet is disturbed by police sirens right outside our window. The local constabulary is leading the bride and groom we spotted on the riverbank back to our hotel, the location for their reception. We get to hear their guests enjoying themselves half the night!

Irkutsk is a terrific city. We enjoy the sights, the old buildings, the broad streets. We are loving this part of Russia a lot more than we expected to.

Brian: Before we head to Listvyanka on the western shore of Lake Baikal I need to find a tyre. The rear Heidenau I put on in Helsinki is splitting and I'm not confident it will make it all the way to Vladivostok. Ken and Carol keep meticulous notes of everywhere they visit and, lucky for us, even have the GPS coordinates for the local Irkutsk tyre retailer. Carol also remembers it is next to a burnt-out building. Sure enough the tyre shop is right next door to a burnt shell that was once a major retail store. They don't have Heidenau tyres but they have a local Mitas brand. It is super cheap, just US$114 and should get us to Vladivostok.

They don't fit tyres here, but he has a friend nearby who can help. All we have to do is get the tyre to the 'big tyre' on the highway. Fully loaded there's not a lot of space on the bike so I jam the tyre onto the bags on the side of the tank. It's very precarious, but should hold as long as the 'big tyre' isn't too far away and too hard to find. The 'big tyre' is actually the size of a house. No problem finding it.

The fitters interrupt smoko to help us out for the equivalent of US$2. In 20 minutes we're on our way to the lake.

•

Lake Baikal is massive. Its shoreline is about 2000 kilometres and it's more than 600 kilometres from tip to tip. At its deepest, the lake is more than 1600 metres. Everyone raves about the views across the lake and the brilliant colours of the water itself. Unluckily for us, the lake is shrouded in smoke haze from the fires on the other side and we can't see the mountains that line the eastern shore.

There's more smoke in the little town itself, but this is coming from the cookers set up at just about every back gate along the road. Locals are smoking and selling fish. Rather than this little morsel we head to the Legend of Lake Baikal Hotel and have lunch on the deck at the water's edge. The seafood salad is delicious. It's just a real shame we don't get to see this natural masterpiece at its best.

•

Our hotel is not the easiest to find. We have to ride around the back of a Soviet style apartment building, through a gate, past the local fire brigade and then scramble up a hillside. On a clear day it would have great views from this high vantage point over the lake. The wind finally blows the smoke away from us and we glimpse the beauty of this amazing body of water.

It's wedding season in Russia and our hotel has a wedding reception in the dining room. We get our meal served in our room and spend the night watching a Harry Potter movie dubbed into Russian. It's an experience.

There is no road on the other side of the lake, just a railway line with a small train chugging along the foreshore, so we have to ride back into Irkutsk and then skirt the southern edge of the lake, riding through the hills.

When we leave it's drizzling rain. I don't mind. In some ways it suits this area. I might come back here one day. There's a challenge in winter when this massive lake freezes and bikers take out Ural sidecars and ride across. It might take a bit of talking to get Shirl to do that.

The ride around the southern side of Baikal takes us up into the foothills with glimpses of the lake below. We trickle through small villages until we come to an escarpment with 180-degree views of the lake. I pull up and we share a snack and just admire the view for a while.

The road then takes us down onto the lake edge before we finally leave it behind and head to Ulan Ude across the now familiar flat plains of Siberia.

Shirl is going to be in her element here. It's the home of the world's largest Lenin head.

Shirley: Our hotel is massive, another former Intourist hotel from the

Soviet days, it is close to the main square and the Mongolian embassy, two things we want in Ulan Ude.

The hotel's name, Buryatiya, isn't easy to recognise in the Cyrillic alphabet and I have to ask an Englishman waiting to check in, just to make sure we're at the right place. Graham is a well-dressed 60-something traveller who has left the Trans-Siberian railway to explore the city for a couple of days before rejoining the train for the last leg to Vladivostok.

Our first job is to get our Mongolian visas. Everyone tells us it is 'across the road'. Well, it is actually across the road, down the hill a bit and behind a shopping centre and vacant block of land. It does stand out, once you see it, with its roofline reminiscent of a Mongolian hat.

We are expecting to wait a couple of days for our visa and are pleasantly surprised when the consul tells us to wait. Half an hour later we leave, nearly US$200 poorer for the fast service, but with our visas.

•

Ulan Ude is alive with family groups making the most of the Siberian summer holiday season before the harsh winter hits, possibly in a few weeks.

The fountain in the square outside the impressive ballet theatre is dancing to classical music. Ice-cream sellers are doing a roaring trade and family groups savour the sweet treats while they enjoy the sunshine and the music. We while away an hour soaking up the atmosphere, but Lenin's head is calling me.

Across the road in Ulan Ude's main square stands the seven-metre-high bronze Lenin head. It's an odd thing, but this huge statue was erected only in the 1970s to commemorate what would have been Lenin's 100th birthday. I am besotted. Some locals say Lenin looks more Asian than European. Others say he is cross-eyed. I don't see it.

The school year begins tomorrow and children are rehearsing a performance to celebrate the end of the holidays. We are enjoying their gymnastic and dance performances. They are enthralled by Brian's beard.

Brian: We've bumped into cars competing in Mongolian rallies throughout Central Asia. One rally actually finished here, in Siberia,

The world's largest Lenin head, Ulan Ude

Ulan Ude

Horse and donkey rides - all part of the summer festival, Ulan Ude
Russian biker gave us weather advice on the road to Mongolia - winter is coming!

because the Mongolian government got sick of competitors abandoning their cars at the end of the gruelling drive from London to the capital, Ulaanbaatar.

There are a couple of Aussies who have competed on MZ 125cc motorcycles. Not satisfied with taking the most direct route across Kazakhstan, they detoured to find the old missile silos, once loaded with Inter-Continental ballistic missiles and nuclear warheads, ready for an attack during the Cold War. As well as carrying all their gear and some spares they also travelled with some rope so they could abseil into the now-abandoned silos. That is a gutsy effort and their photos are amazing.

•

We can't resist another ice-cream in the square outside the ballet theatre. Today children are riding toy horses around the fountain. They are ingenious. The kids put pressure on the stirrups and the little horses move around. I wonder what the kids in Australia would think of a simple pleasure like this in comparison to their iPads and video games.

•

It's our last night in Russia for a few days. We're heading into Mongolia tomorrow. We can't leave Ulan Ude without dining in Churchill's bar, directly opposite Lenin's head.

Decked out like an English pub it's a little piece of home for Graham, who is rejoining the train tomorrow. It is fine English pub fare – bangers and mash, steak and chips – and they serve English beer and European wines.

At the next table are the two Aussies from the rally. Part of me is envious because they will be home in a couple of days, but part of me is keen to continue on our ride. Tomorrow Mongolia and then a long ride across Siberia to Vladivostok lies ahead of us.

Mongolia

2 – 7 September 2015

Brian: There's no option but to be up and about early today. The hotel's power is being turned off and it would be a long walk down from the 8th floor, and we've got a 250-kilometre ride to get to the Mongolian border.

It's cool this morning, but not unbearable. It's hard to imagine that in winter the temperature plummets to more than 20°C below and even Lake Baikal freezes over.

We pass a motorcyclist heading back to Ulan Ude. He waves and pulls over so we do a U-turn and join him on the side of the road. We still don't speak much Russian, but through his limited English and charades we learn that we must hurry to Vladivostok because winter is coming and it is coming fast. He also tells us that the Ulaanbaatar traffic is dreadful. Bad traffic doesn't faze us. We've ridden through some cities where the drivers have no consideration for motorcycles and can clearly be described as homicidal. The Mongolian traffic can't be any worse. Surely not.

We exchange stickers and head on our way – him to his home in Northern Siberia and us to Mongolia.

•

We've been warned that the border here closes for lunch. I'm relieved we get to the Russian side at 11.30am. An official asks for the paperwork we were given when we left Kazakhstan. Oops. We don't have anything. This could be a problem.

I am led away, leaving Shirl and the bike at the border immigration office. I follow the official into a modern, air-conditioned building. Even though he seems pretty friendly, I'm fearful that we've managed to create a major problem for ourselves.

Inside the building I'm led into an office where a young Russian

Welcome to Mongolia

On the road to Ulaanbaatar

Animals graze along the road to Ulaanbaatar

Buddhist Stupas

woman in uniform asks me to sit. We then go through every date of our arrivals and departures into and out of Russia. I need to remember the date we arrived in Russia from Finland, when we left for Kazakhstan and then when we returned from Kazakhstan just a couple of weeks ago. Using my passport as a prompt we sort out the dates and the form is filled in.

Apparently Kazakhstan has only recently become part of the Russian Federation and the border guards probably weren't aware of their responsibilities. I remember when they took our original entry form and didn't return it to me, but thought nothing of it at the time.

The form is a statuary declaration kind of document. I have to swear that these are the dates we crossed the Russian border with the motorcycle. I then need to explain why we don't have the paperwork. The form is completed in English and I sign it. All correct.

As we walk back to Shirl and the bike I'm assured that we'll be right to return to Russia after our quick trip to Mongolia and the paperwork will be correct to get the motorcycle out of Russia when we leave Vladivostok. The border guards and officials couldn't be more friendly or helpful. Thank you.

Shirl is obviously relieved when I get back. Standing there, for probably nearly an hour, she must have been thinking the worst.

Our passports are stamped and we're on our way, through no man's land, to Mongolia only to find the gates are closed.

A woman in uniform comes out of the quarantine area and yells out to someone we can't see. The gatehouse door opens and a man emerges, wiping the remnants of his lunch from his lips onto his palms and then wipes his hands on his trousers. He pushes the metal gate open and beckons for us to come in. He gives our paperwork a cursory glance and signals for us to head over to the passport control area inside the compound. As he walks back to the gatehouse and his lunch he looks back over his shoulder and says, 'Welcome to Mongolia'. Thanks.

The paperwork is simple. A couple of stamps and we are in Mongolia. With the help of some truckies waiting to get into Russia, we find the insurance office and the ATM. Cashed up and armed with the insurance for the motorcycle we are through and on the road to Darkhan.

Shirley: We probably have time to ride straight to Ulaanbaatar, about 400 kilometres away, but, if we make good time, we'll arrive in the capital at peak hour. Let's not test out the warning about the bad drivers at the busiest time of the day.

It's only 240 kilometres to Darkhan where we've been told there's a good hotel, so that's where we head.

The Mongolian countryside is just what we imaged – rolling green hills, pastures with horses, sheep, goats and even yaks grazing alongside yurts.

There are Buddhist stupas nestled along the hillsides. This is a bit of a surprise. During the Soviet years the communists destroyed the monasteries and murdered the monks or sent them to Siberian labour camps. Mongolians were only able to begin practising their favoured religion again in 1990.

•

The Comfort Hotel comes highly recommended but it is comfort in name only. The bed is the hardest we've encountered. It's like sleeping on the floor, and even the floor might be a bit softer!

It is a beautiful afternoon. The sun is shining and the breeze is warm. We get a table at the outdoor restaurant and peruse the menu. There are some interesting local delicacies on offer – liver served with lamb's tails, and horse rectum. Thanks, but no thanks. We opt for a bowl of pasta and a cold local beer.

Brian's 60th birthday is coming up and I'd like to organise a special treat for him so I'm planning to organise premium economy airline tickets home. After some of the hard riding it will be quite luxurious. I have terrible trouble keeping a secret! He gets emotional when we start talking about home. I'm not the only who misses our family. His Mum turns 80 later this month and I know he'd like to get home in time to surprise her.

We are on the downward stretch now. It's time to start planning getting the bike and us home from Vladivostok.

•

The ride from Darkhan to Ulaanbaatar is just as beautiful as yesterday. More rolling hills and grazing herds. I haven't seen so many shades of green since we were in Ireland.

About 20 kilometres from the capital the smog settles in the valleys.

Marco Polo, Ulaanbaatar

Genghis Khan, Ulaanbaatar

The Beatles Square, Ulaanbaatar

Gandantegchenling Monastery, Ulaanbaatar

Dinner at Mexikhan Restaurant with Elad, Ricardo, Bryn and Mihai, Ulaanbaatar

The closer we get the thicker the air becomes. From the pristine air of the countryside we are heading into a smoggy city.

Brian: I really don't enjoy riding into big cities and the smog in the air doesn't auger well for an enjoyable ride the rest of the way to the capital. We hit a major roundabout and seem to be in the suburbs. The green hills are replaced with concrete buildings, symbols from the austere days of communism.

The traffic is pretty heavy but not so bad until we get to the outskirts of the city. Now it's bedlam. We take about an hour and a half to travel just 10 kilometres. The drivers cut across in front of us, try to push us out of our lane, blast their horns when I stand my ground. We narrowly avoid being rear-ended and rear-ending cars that stop suddenly for no apparent reason. The stories we've heard are true, but perhaps a little understated. Ulaanbaatar, you win my award for the world's worst drivers. I never realised it could be this bad!

My temper is at boiling point when the GPS directs us off the main road and down a series of side streets, only to take us back onto the same main road. This completely unnecessary detour does my head in. The chequered flag signalling our hotel is so close, just down the next back street.

A policeman signals for me to pull over, but I ignore his frantic hand signals and head down the street and into our hotel's carpark. I'm thankful we didn't ride here yesterday. If this is just mid-afternoon traffic, what must peak hour be like?

Shirley: Brian does a remarkable job getting through the heavy city traffic. We've arrived with plenty of time to stock up on supplies, taking advantage of the fridge in our room.

There's an underpass to get across the main street, Peace Avenue, to the supermarket. We load up on cheese, biscuits, fruit and yogurt, some local beers and a bottle of European wine. The local speciality is the Genghis Khan vodka. At around US$4 a bottle it is incredibly good. We don't need to head out to dinner tonight.

The hotel has English language news television channels. A dose of international news while sipping local vodka is not a bad way to spend the night.

•

There's no dusty after-effects from the vodka. We are both revived after a good night's sleep and ready to tackle Ulaanbaatar on foot. We've been warned about pickpockets, particularly in this tourist area but don't feel intimidated or threatened in any way.

Walking down Peace Avenue, we head to Genghis Khan Square. Modern buildings line the wide boulevard. Marco Polo, who travelled through the country in the 1200s, is commemorated on the edge of the square with a very impressive statue.

Born in the 12th Century, Genghis is revered by the Mongolian people. His statue, erected to commemorate the 800th anniversary of his coronation, sits above the square, flanked by Mongolian soldiers. The square is decorated with topiary bushes, shaped to represent animals, surrounding a statue of local hero, Sukhbaatar, who freed the country from the Chinese with the assistance of Soviet Russia.

•

Further down Peace Avenue we see a sign for Mary and Martha's, a fair trade souvenir shop that we've been told is the best place to buy something unique to send home. Tucked up a laneway, the shop is the Aladdin's Cave of Mongolian handicrafts. Embroidery by local indigenous men and women has been made into bags of all shapes and sizes from something to carry your phone to tote bags and overnight bags. There are felt miniatures perfect for Christmas decorations and even a ger (called a yurt in other parts of Central Asia) egg cosy.

A friend once told me that she buys small trinkets to hang on the Christmas tree when she's travelling. It's something I now do, too. I've purchased special ornaments in Norway, Finland and Russia on this trip. And now I have a ger to hang on the tree.

The *pièce de résistance* is the vintage wall hangings, hand-embroidered by Mongolian Kazakhs from the far west of the country. These unique pieces are all at least 25 years old and once hung inside a Kazakh ger. The very patient store manager spreads out several of the hangings for us to choose from. It's a hard decision and we don't want to make a mistake with our choice. The hangings are 2.3 x 1.5 metres and will be very prominent in whichever room it hangs at home.

Pieces of these wall hangings have been made into cushion covers – another perfect present to take home for others. The camel hair socks

Монгол хоол / Mongolian food

ЦӨЦГИЙТЭЙ ШАРСАН БАНШ | FRIED DUMPLING SOUP 10500
үхрийн мах, шөлтэй, гурил,ногооны хачир

БУУЗ | BUUZ 10000
гарчир татсан мах, ногооны салат

ЦУЙВАН | TSUIWAN 9900
хонины мах, сүүл, лууван, байцаа

ХУУШУУР | KHUUSHUUR 12900
гарчир татсан мах, ногооны хачир

ШАРСАН ЭЛЭГ, СҮҮЛТЭЙ | FRIED LIVER WITH LAMB TAIL 9500
үхрийн элэг, сүүл, тваа, ногооны хачир

ТӨМӨР ДЭЭР ШАРСАН ХОНИНЫ МАХ | FRIED MUTTON ON THE IRON PLATE 16500
хонины мах, төмс, лууван, будаа, хачир

ҮХРИЙН ЧАНАСАН ХАВИРГА | BOVINE COSTA 19000
хавирга, гурил, төмс, лууван, манжин

АДУУНЫ ЧАНАСАН МАХ—УМС ХИТАЙ | HORSE RECTUM 18000
адууны мах, умс, хитай, гурил, чанасан ногоо

ХОРХОГ | KHORKHOG IS A DISH IN MONGOLIAN CUISINE 22000
хонины мах, чанасан ногоо, шөл

ХОНИНЫ ЧАНАСАН ӨВЧҮҮ | BOVINE BREAST PIECE 28000
өвчүү, гурил, чанасан ногоо

НОГООТОЙ ХУУШУУР | KHUUSHUUR WITH VEGETABLES 8900
аниуй, мөөг, чинжүү, төмс, лууван

НОГООТОЙ БАНШ | DUMPLING WITH VEGETABLES 8900
аниуй, мөөг, чинжүү, төмс, лууван, цөцгий

ЖИМБИЙ | ROAST LAMB WITH ROLLED DOUGH 20000
хонины мах, гурил, чанасан ногоо, шөл

Уух зүйлс / Drink

Сүүтэй цай	Milk tea 800
Хөөрүүлсэн сүү	Boiled milk 2000
Ларцтай будаа	Curds with rice 3900
Айраг	Airag 2000
Шимийн архи	Milk Vodka 5000

Mongolian specialities, Darkhan

Genghis Khan statue

are much softer than you'd expect and Brian can't resist the yak wool socks.

We buy up big because this parcel of goodies will be posted home with the help of the Mary and Martha's girls. One of the shop assistants who speaks very good English is assigned to go with us to the post office and help us. With her help our parcel is boxed, addressed, weighed and dispatched for home in about 20 minutes.

All this shopping has worked up an appetite and we head to the City Restaurant, across the avenue from the post office for a spectacular Chinese meal. We won't need dinner again tonight.

Brian: Bryn, Ricardo and Elad, whom we last saw in Barnaul, are in town. We were going to leave tomorrow, but a decision to stay another day and ride out to the Genghis Khan statue with them is made in a split second. Dinner arrangements are made before we head out for another day in Ulaanbaatar.

Shirl has read about the Winter Palace and we ask for directions at the hotel but somehow end up at the city's main Buddhist monastery. We walk around the complex and watch people praying at the stupas and prayer wheels. It's very serene. That's something we've noticed everywhere in the world – where there are Buddhists the world is calm.

In the main temple is the Migjid Janraisig statue. It's 26 metres high and Shirl decides to pay the extra fee to use her camera. Admission to the temple is 5000 Mongolian tughrik (about AUD$3.40). The monk on the door charges her 10,000 tughrik for the camera. Within a second of taking her first photo another monk asks for her ticket. She doesn't have one. She must pay 7000 for the camera. When she tells him she already paid 10,000 he shrugs and wanders off. Surely she hasn't been ripped off by a Buddhist monk?

The statue towers over us in its golden glory. It's probably worth paying about AUD$6.80 for the privilege of getting the photos. I'm sure she was born to be a tourist!

Wandering back down Peace Avenue we make a detour to Beatles Square, where John, Paul George and Ringo are commemorated in stone. Apparently in the 1970s young Mongolians would hide in the laneways and stairwells of this part of the city and sing Beatles hits learned from contraband records smuggled in from Europe. Another photo op for my girl.

•

At the end of a long day walking around the city we head out to Mexikhan Restaurant – I just love a pun! The Mexican eatery comes highly recommended by Ken and Carol and doesn't disappoint.

Ricardo, Bryn and Elad arrive with another rider who is staying at their guesthouse. As soon as he walks in the door we recognise him – Mihai, the Romanian we met at the Moscow Café in Dushanbe, Tajikistan. It's that small world thing again!

Mexikhan is a modern restaurant with a mezzanine floor and a well-stocked bar. I get talking to two Aussies and an American who are working in the local mining industry. They give me some good advice about eating in countries without major refrigeration – only ever eat small animals.

'A chicken they will kill, cook and eat on the same day. A larger beast, a horse or goat, they will kill and cook and then cook again and then again. The smaller the animal the fresher the meat will be.'

It makes sense.

Ricardo, Bryn and Elad have ridden across Western Mongolia rather than heading south from Ulan Ude. The roads have been difficult – sandy tracts and major water crossings. The tracks are impossible to find without GPS and even difficult with the coordinates. I'm happy with our decision to ride into the capital from the north.

Shirley: We meet the boys at their guesthouse for the ride to the Genghis Khan statue, about 50 kilometres out of town. The road is sealed all the way, so it should be an easy ride.

Mihai has a hangover after a night drinking with some German backpackers he bumped into after leaving dinner. Foolishly we let him lead the ride to the statue.

He takes a turn off the good sealed road and we head overland past tiny houses and bemused locals. A track appears and we follow that for a while, dodging rocks and weaving our way around sandpits and trying to avoid the worst of the road. Then it stops altogether. After a quick conversation we head back overland and make our way across a narrow creek and back onto the main road. It was an interesting detour I could probably have lived without!

Genghis Khan statue

Giant boot at Genghis Khan statue

Riding out with Bryn, Mihai, Elad and Ricardo

Buddhist Stupas

Not far along the sealed road we come to roadworks and are diverted over a very sandy track that is congested with traffic. The swirling dust means we can't see more than a few metres. This statue better be worth it!

Finally, we're on the right road and a dense fog descends. Maybe we're not meant to see Genghis Khan today. After all of this I don't want to get there and not be able to see the statue.

We couldn't be more wrong. The fog lifts, revealing blue sky and sunshine. And there, glistening in the sun, is Genghis Khan - towering 40 metres into the sky on horseback with whip and sword. Magnificent. He is made from stainless steel, so no wonder he shimmers.

Inside the base of the statue is a traditional Mongolian boot, but standing nine metres high. The museum houses the most incredible collection of Genghis Khan memorabilia dating back to the 1200s – buttons, buckles, jewellery, swords, steel helmets – amazing stuff.

We take the lift into the statue and walk up the steep steps to the viewing platform under the horse's head. Genghis Khan looks out over his kingdom. We are all very impressed!

•

It is time to say farewell – again. Ricardo and Elad are leaving their bikes here and flying home in the next couple of days. Mihai is going to hang around a bit longer. Bryn will ride to Darkhan with us in the morning when we head back to Ulan Ude.

Brian: After the dreadful traffic on our ride into Ulaanbaatar I'm determined to miss the morning traffic on Peace Avenue. I've been told about a ring road that will take us out of town, avoiding the gridlock.

Bryn follows as I try and find the mysterious ring road. At every turn there are traffic jams, made worse by water sitting on the road from overnight storms.

Eventually we hit Peace Avenue, less than a kilometre from our hotel and it's taken us about 40 minutes to get here.

Bugger me if the traffic on Peace Avenue is moving smoothly, without any holdups. The ride to avoid the avenue was the worst part of the ride out of town.

•

We ride back past the Buddhist stupas, past rolling green hills, pastures and their animals.

Today is probably the coldest day we've had since we left Scandinavia, down to 12°C. The air is crisp and clean. It's perfect riding weather.

Bryn is heading to Lake Baikal and will continue on towards the border today.

We break the journey at Darkhan again and head back to the uncomfortable Comfort Hotel.

The three of us share a late lunch/early dinner in a ger restaurant. We avoid the lamb's tails and horse rectum.

Tomorrow we'll cross back into Russia and begin our last ride through Siberia.

We're on the home straight.

Mongolian herder

Buddhism began to flourish in Mongolia again in 1990

Eastern Siberia
Ulan Ude to Vladivostok

8 – 16 September 2015

Brian: It's only a short ride to the border this morning and I want to get there early. The officials assured us the paperwork for the bike will be OK but I want to get there in plenty of time, just in case.

On the Mongolian side everything is going well until the young female official tries to key in the details for the motorcycle. She can't work it out and calls over a man who tries but also has problems.

After a few minutes everyone in the customs office has left their posts and all five are giving advice on how the details can be keyed in. This doesn't auger well when you consider we are leaving Mongolia not trying to get into the country.

When they finally have success we take a detour through the duty-free store to spend the last of our Mongolia currency. The only thing we can afford are two bottle openers bearing the Mongolian flag. We are actually 50 tugrik short but the young lady lets us go. We are her only customers and 50 tugrik is the equivalent to less than five cents so I don't think it is going to have a bearing on the state of the Mongolian economy.

With all of the mucking around and our visit to duty free it's taken us 45 minutes to leave Mongolia. That is quite a long time leaving a country.

On the Russian side, the queue is snaking its way several hundred metres along the driveway, ending at the border post itself. Shirl solves the mystery of why there are so many people crossing into Russia this morning. There is a Cash and Carry store just outside the border gates and many Mongolians come across here to shop.

The paperwork is all fine for us, but then there is a hiccup with the bike's paperwork. No one has noticed before, but our bike is registered in a company name. The vigilant official at this crossing wants to know why I have the bike and it is not registered in my name.

We have a letter translated into Russian, giving me permission to have the bike outside of Australia. On the advice of Mick McDonald from Compass Expeditions, who has done many rides across Russia, we have put our company stamp on the letter a couple of times. The Russians love stamps and this letter does the trick. Another stamp and we are back in Russia.

Riding out I can hear Shirl singing into her helmet Back in the USSR, made famous by the Beatles and Billy Joel. Even though she seems to know all the words I'm glad she hasn't been serenading me every time we've crossed into Russia.

Shirley: *Flew in from Miami Beach BOAC,*
didn't get to bed last night
On the way the paper bag was on my knee,
man I had a dreadful flight.
I'm back in the USSR ...

Sorry Brian. I can't resist.

It's an uneventful ride back to Ulan Ude, but what a difference a week makes. The Summer festival is over. Gone are the red and white lights in the square. The fountain is no longer flood lit and the music has been silenced. There is a chill in the air. Winter is definitely coming.

We do one last lap around Lenin's head and have another meal in Churchill's bar before we begin the ride along the Trans-Siberian Highway to the east coast.

We are now on the downward run to Vladivostok. The 'go to' freight agent in Vlad, Yuri Melnik, has told us he can't get the bike to Australia but will do all the paperwork to get it out of Russia to South Korea. Brian has been emailing a couple of shipping agents in South Korea without a lot of luck so far. They have a long weekend coming up and everything will be closed for a few days. This will delay getting the bike onto a ship to come home. The South Korean holiday is putting a spanner in the works.

We've had an amazing time on this trip, but it's time to go home now and if we can get back in time for the surprise it will be perfect.

Brian: It is a cold and windy day today. The wind is bringing in the rain. We have more than 600 kilometres to get to Chita, our overnight stop. The main highway, the M55 was 700 kilometres plus so we take the shorter route, marked as a secondary road on the map.

The road is no different from any of the other Russian roads. Sometimes it's really good and sometimes it's really bad. It was a pleasure riding on the stretch of road from Ulan Ude to the Mongolian border with no roadworks. I guess Siberia is like Alaska – they need to complete roadworks in the summer months when there is no snow to hamper their progress.

Today we hit a long stretch of roadworks in the rain and it's treacherous. The trucks are churning up the mud, making for a slippery ride, made more nerve-wracking by the car that sits right up our backside. The driver has no idea. If I slip in this mud he'll run right over us. Luckily, with a bit of wrestling, we get through without dropping the bike.

Shirley: I hold my breath while we ride through sloppy mud like these roadworks. Brian does a remarkable job, but I have to admit I dread days like today.

It's a long, cold, wet ride and we are both looking forward to a hot shower when we get to Chita, our overnight stop. Because of its proximity to China and military installations, this city was closed to foreigners and most Russians from the 1930s until the collapse of the USSR.

Chita is on the Trans-Siberian railway route, 900 kilometres from Irkutsk. We are making good progress, heading east, now. Riding into the town the hand of the Soviets is clear. The highway is lined with apartment blocks that are best described as concrete monoliths. Some have been dollied up with little balconies but most are as they were – bleak.

Our hotel, in the middle of one of these concrete residential areas, has bi-lingual staff – speaking Russian and Chinese. While this makes checking in a little tricky it bodes well for dinner, with a Chinese restaurant on the first floor of the building.

The hotel is under renovation and our room is sparkling and comfy, but the water isn't hot which is a bit disappointing after such a cold ride. We crank up the heating to warm us up and dry out our gloves and boots. Ah, the joys of life on the road!

The restaurant doesn't disappoint and a menu complete with beautiful photos of the meals to tempt our tastebuds ordering is easy. It's a cracker of a meal.

•

Breakfast is just as good – light, thin pancakes served with condensed milk to pour over the top. It's probably not the healthiest meal but it is so sweet and so delicious – who cares? Not us!

The first largish town on the highway today is Chernyshevsky but it doesn't have anything that looks remotely interesting for us to bother stopping. I read about a hotel in the town but it has no shower and a shared toilet. It's only 1pm when we hit the outskirts and a short ride down the dirt track that leads into the town makes us realise this isn't the town for us and it's too early to stop for the day anyway.

We have enough fuel to get to the next town, Mogocha, only about 230 kilometres away. We'll fuel up there and, hopefully, get a room for the night. TripAdvisor has two hotels listed in the centre of the town. We just need to find them.

•

The clouds gather late in the day and down comes the rain by the bucketload. On the highway at the Mogocha turn off we've got about 80 kilometre range in the petrol tank. This is cutting it a bit fine.

The GPS indicates a fuel stop on the edge of the town but we can't find it so we head into town. It's raining, gloomy and the town looks depressed and depressing. We can't see anything that looks like a hotel, but fuel has to be our first priority.

Brian: As we ride down a street a small, clapped-out old Lada pulls alongside us. Like so many cars in this part of Russia it is a right-hand drive. The driver winds down the window and a huge fug of smoke rolls out. A hand appears with a cigarette clenched between the fingers. The driver shouts something at us.

'What did he say?' I ask Shirl.

'It sounded like clubhouse – follow me.'

And so I do.

The Lada weaves its way down narrow side streets, past a school and small houses until it stops outside a simple, wooden building that looks a little like an American barn. On the wall above the double doors is a stylised image of a motorcyclist.

We have arrived at the Mogocha Iron Angels clubhouse.

The driver of the car and his passenger leap out and wrench open the double doors and signal that I should ride the bike inside. The ramp is reasonably steep, but it is sealed so I gun the engine and ride up.

Alexei, the vice-president, is a man in his 50s who certainly doesn't look like a big tough bikie. He is wearing glasses and his thinning hair hangs down over his forehead. With him is Sasha, a younger, taller and fitter-looking man. He's a biker from Vladivostok and is on his way home. He's has been staying at the clubhouse for the past couple of nights.

These bikers are certainly not the one-percenters we see in Australia riding their Harleys and wearing patches declaring their club membership.

They are friendly, working-class blokes who enjoy riding motorcycles during the summer months, before the biting winter hits their Siberian town.

The clubhouse is a two-storey shed, really, built by the members as a place for bikers to stay when riding the vast distances across Siberia. After the murder of a friend who was camping in the forest they built the clubhouse so riders would have a safe place to stay.

We introduce ourselves and Alexei welcomes us to Mogocha. Sasha speaks much better English than the vice-president and he interprets for us.

Shirley: Once the bike is tucked away downstairs Alexei goes upstairs and tells us to follow. Well, it's not stairs, more a ladder. It's steep and each step is a different height and a different width. I manage to trip up the last one and make a most ungraceful entrance into the upper room, much to everyone's amusement.

There is a table covered in empty bottles, dirty glasses, an overflowing ashtray and a loaf of bread in the centre of the room, with three couches around it. There is another table in the corner with an assortment of dishes and paper cups.

In a corner there's a large container of water, a computer, a portable gas stove and a pile of books and magazines. On top is a Russian/English dictionary.

Alexei asks if we need food. I explain that I need a toilet. Sasha tells me there is no toilet. There isn't even running water.

Oh.

They suggest we head into town for something to eat. There is a toilet there.

Good idea.

The four of us pile into Alexei's rickety old car and end up at the local supermarket where there is a small café and toilets that are my first port of call.

We've heard so much about Russian hospitality and we see it first-hand here in Mogocha. We have a very hearty vegetable soup and dumplings that Sasha tells us are a local favourite. When I bite into one the oil flows out over my hand. They are a bit oily but very tasty. The soup is incredibly filling.

Alexei sends Sasha off to get money out of the automatic bank and refuses to take any money from us. We are their guests and guests do not pay.

While Brian and Sasha talk bikes I sneak off to the supermarket and get some vodka, wine, water, Coke and snacks. Always thinking of my next meal, I even throw in a couple of tubs of yogurt for breakfast. We load our purchases into the Lada and head back to the clubhouse. Sasha and Alexei have three bottles of local beer that comes in two-litre plastic bottles.

Brian: The beer is pretty damn good and we are working our way through the first bottle when I hear a few bikes pull up outside. Alexei heads downstairs and we can hear a very animated conversation in Russian. A few minutes pass and Alexei comes back with another biker. Francisco is younger, probably in his 20s. His hair is cut in a Mohawk style. He looks chilled to the bone. It's dark outside and still raining. Francisco tells us he met up with members of the club on the highway and they've brought him here to spend the night.

Alexei fires up the stove and heats up a stew that's been sitting in the pot for goodness knows how long. Francisco hops into it, washed down with a glass of the wine. He and the president then crack open the vodka.

Churchill's Bar, Ulan Ude

One last look at Lenin, Ulan Ude

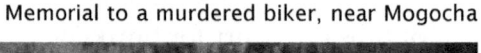

Memorial to a murdered biker, near Mogocha

Brian with Sasha and Alexei at the Mogocha Iron Angels clubhouse

For the next couple of hours we talk more about bikes and toast all manner of events and people before throwing down shots of vodka. Shirl is sipping quietly on her wine, just taking it all in. When I ask if she is OK she says she doesn't want to consume too much liquid because of the toilet situation – probably a good idea.

Alexei, with the help of Sasha and his dog-eared dictionary, tells us the sad tale of his friend, Alexei Barsukov, who disappeared while camping in the Siberian forest. The story goes that a crazy man stumbled onto his campsite and wanted him to drink vodka. The biker didn't drink but that wasn't good enough for the intruder. Insulted because his offer of vodka was refused, he murdered the biker.

For days Alexei and other club members searched for their friend, finally finding his body hidden among the trees. Alexei tells us the murderer was helped by a local businessman to avoid arrest. Strangely, his business burnt to the ground after the murderer was captured. A little case of summary justice, I think.

Alexei is clearly moved by the loss of his friend. Tears well and slowly run down his cheeks.

The club has erected a monument in his honour, near where he met his death. You get the feeling this is Alexei's finest achievement. Each year bikers from all over Russia meet at the monument to remember their friend.

This explains the clubhouse. Bikers no longer camp in the forest. They come and sleep here. It might be a little shabby but it is safe and we have a warm and dry room to lay our heads tonight.

As the night wears on, Alexei's son comes to take him home. He won't be driving the little Lada tonight.

Shirley: Brian stands guard while I take a pee in the garden at the back of the building. Sasha and Francisco say we should have the most comfortable couch because we are the married couple – read for this 'old'. It's a folded down 'night and day' vinyl couch that reminds me of the one we had at home in the 1960s. It may be the exact model!

Francisco is hammered and as he drops off to sleep he shouts 'don't ever drink with Australians'. That makes me laugh considering who was drinking the vodka – the Russians and the Spaniard.

Snuggled down in our sleeping bags I am very grateful we are here.

A clubhouse with no running water and no toilet isn't my ideal overnight stop but there is no doubt the Mogocha Iron Angels saved us. Thank you Alexei.

Brian: We're up well before Sasha and Francisco. In the daylight there isn't actually a spot in the unfenced garden where Shirl can have a pee without being seen by everyone passing by. I stand guard again, luckily no one comes.

We pack up and wait for the others to surface. We want to leave some money to thank Alexei and Sasha for their hospitality. Without them we would have been stuffed. There's a fishbowl at the top of the stairs with some cash in it. I add to it, ensuring it is enough to cover what they outlaid. It is the least we can do.

We're all heading the same way today, towards Svobodnyy, and we'll ride with Sasha and Francisco part of the way. We plan to stop at a new motel on the highway Ken and Carol told us about, near Magdagachi, a town we've been advised to avoid. Not just Ken and Carol, but other travellers we've met have described it as a 'bad' town and unsafe for visitors, but no one can explain why.

The boys are heading to another bike clubhouse. I think we'd rather a comfortable bed and a shower tonight.

•

The Coke that Shirl bought last night is consumed with gusto by the others to ease the hangovers that are very obvious.

Our first stop is the supermarket and the toilets. Second stop is fuel. It is in the general area our GPS tried to direct us to last night, but hidden behind a tin fence. No wonder we missed it in the dark and rain.

It's a very basic fuel station, with the petrol in tanks controlled by a woman who is inside a shed with only a tiny window to look out on her patch. Like so many of these women working in such harsh conditions, she is less than helpful, but Shirl perseveres and we manage to get *polni* – a full tank.

•

Sasha takes the lead and stops at the memorial to the biker murdered in the forest. The Iron Angels have done a remarkable job remembering their friend. His memorial is black marble and adorned with stickers

Overlooking China, Blagoveshchensk

Great Patriotic War memorial, Blagoveshchensk

Vladivostok

Lenin, Blagoveshchensk

Aleksandr Solzhenitsyn, Vladivostok

placed there by motorcyclists from around the world who have stopped to pay their respects. There is one of Ken and Carol's and another from the SR 500 Club, a Melbourne group we've got to know pretty well in recent years. We add ours to the collection.

Sasha tells us the murdered man had a family – a wife and children – who are now without a father and a husband just because he refused to drink vodka. It is a poignant moment for all four of us.

•

The road is a good one for a change. We stop a couple of times when Sasha and Francisco stop for a smoke and to fuel up. Even the service stations are better, selling good food as well as fuel.

I explain that we are looking for a new motel near the turn off to Magdagachi and Sasha says we shouldn't stay there. He's OK when I tell him the motel isn't in the town, it's on the highway.

Shirley: We ride past what looks to me like the motel we've been looking for, but it is nowhere near the turn-off to Magdagachi. That's nearly 100 kilometres away. The next sign we see is for the turn-off to the town. Sasha and Francisco pull over and we say goodbye, after assuring them we won't be taking the turn, but will continue on to the motel.

Of course, that motel never appears. Obviously we should have stopped at the one more than 100 kilometres back. No way will Brian turn around. We'll just keep going to Svobodnyy. Because we left Mogocha so late and spent nearly half an hour at the memorial it is going to be after 8 o'clock before we get to the town.

It's already dark when we get to the turn off to Svobodnyy. There don't seem to be any towns right on the Trans-Siberian Highway. Brian turns and puts the hammer down. We have another 40 kilometres to ride.

He overtakes the slower drivers and then catches up with a car that is also in a hurry. Using it as a guide he rides pretty quickly. I know better than to say too much about it.

When we get to the town there is a hotel on the GPS. The receptionist manages to drag herself away from the soap opera on the television and organises a room for us. There's even parking for the bike at the back of the building.

A man meanders outside and gets talking to Brian and shows him how to get to the parking area. I thought he was drunk, but when Brian offers him a beer to thank him for his help he says he doesn't need one.... he's stoned!

Brian: A hot shower, a comfortable bed and we are both feeling refreshed. We don't have far to go today, just to Blagoveshchensk, on the border with China. It's out of our way but we've been told it is well worth the detour.

We arrive mid-afternoon and realise when we were told the town was on the border it wasn't an exaggeration. The river Amur and about 100 metres of no man's land separates Russia from the Chinese town of Heihe and its highrise buildings and Ferris wheel.

We spend a couple of hours wandering through the city and Shirl is in her element. A statue of Lenin takes pride of place in the city centre. He's in his usual pose, with one hand clutching his lapel and the other outstretched, beckoning the faithful.

Chinese visitors jostle to get the best spot to take a photo of their friends with the statue. Someone has placed flowers at Lenin's feet. He might be *persona non grata* in some places but here he is still revered.

As night falls China comes to life in a multitude of colours. The glass and steel structures are transformed into a light show. You get the feeling the Chinese are pointing out to their Russian neighbours how dull their city is by comparison.

•

We are just two days from Vladivostok now. Today we will head to Khabarovsk, an historic town that the guidebook says has dancing fountains, interesting architecture and more Lenin statues.

It is Sunday. The ferry from Vlad to South Korea leaves on Wednesdays and motorcycles are loaded on Tuesdays. If we get to Vladivostok on Monday night, we'll get to South Korea with a few days to spare to lodge the bike before the holiday long weekend shuts down the wharves.

If we don't get the ferry until next week, we'll get tied up in the long weekend and won't get home to Australia until early October and I'll miss Mum's 80th.

I know Shirl is disappointed because Khabarovsk is her kind of town, but she understands how important it is to me to get home. And she wants to get home too.

Moscow to Vladivostok sign

Great Patriotic War memorial, Vladivostok

With Ian, Mike and Christian, Vladivostok   En route from Vladivostok to South Korea

Shirley: We head back to the main road and head to Khabarovsk. We stop at the first fuel station – a wonderful, modern station with very friendly staff. It really makes a difference when the staff aren't locked away in tiny rooms with only a small window to look out.

I'm perusing the well-stocked shelves while I have a drink and one of the young girls working behind the counter comes up and touches my arm to attract my attention. When I turn around she presents me with a fridge magnet of Blagoveshchensk. She is beaming at me. 'This is for you.' What a lovely gesture.

•

We don't ride far before we round a corner and see the iconic Moscow to Vladivostok sign. This massive concrete sign curves around a parking area on the side of the highway. There are trucks parked and some vendors selling local produce in front of it, but we manage to get some photos of the bike with just the sign and a selfie. We both look incredibly happy! And why wouldn't we – the sun is shining and the road is good. This is an achievement – we're close to Vladivostok now. If we'd ridden directly here from Moscow we would have ridden about a third of the distance. We've come the long way!

•

In Khabarovsk we are in a lovely hotel with a comfortable room and a trendy restaurant serving excellent food.

I would have liked to explore this city, but it isn't that important to me. We need to get to Vlad and on to that ferry to South Korea.

Brian: We are on the homeward run now. Our last day on the road in Russia is a good one. We don't encounter any roadworks or potholes. Shirl asks me to pull over. She wants to get the GoPro selfie stick out and get some video of us riding. We've carried this useless piece of kit with us the entire journey and haven't used it once. I guess we should get at least some footage of us with it. We really aren't video people.

The closer we get to Vlad the worse the traffic becomes but that's to be expected. The city is home to a massive university and a bustling sea port.

Not far from the hotel the traffic is gridlocked. There's been a minor nose-to-tail crash and, as is the norm here, the drivers are waiting patiently for the police to come and photograph the scene before they move the cars.

At times like this the bike comes into its own. I ride around the smash, taking to the footpath and end up right outside the door to our hotel.

Inside the foyer is hectic with people checking in and out. I don't pay much attention to a group of men standing to one side until an English voice shouts at us, 'You wouldn't be Brian and Shirley, would you?'

It is Ian Chappell: an Englishman I've been conversing with over the Net for the past couple of months. I've followed his journey with interest. He's tackled the infamous 'Road of Bones', a stretch of road that is said to have been built over the bodies of prisoners from Stalin's Gulags.

He's faced some difficult days on the road but has survived and has just arrived in Vladivostok from Magadan, the town at the end of the Road of Bones. He's with two other travellers he's met along the way – Christian and Mike. They're waiting for their bikes to arrive in town before they can plan the next leg of their rides.

We arrange to meet them for a drink and dinner and end up at a North Korean restaurant, about half an hour's walk from the hotel. They share horror stories of crashes, bad roads and broken bikes that now just elicit laughter. Nothing seems quite as bad when you look back on it.

•

The freight service provided by Yuri takes all the worry out of getting the bike out of Russia. He's booked the bike on to the ferry leaving for Donghae in South Korea tomorrow. We have to lodge the bike this morning and he's at the hotel ready to organise that at 9 o'clock sharp. Shirl goes in the van with Yuri and I follow on the bike.

The first stop is the wharf where we take the bike to the freight holding area alongside the Eastern Dream, our ferry. There's a cash fee of 1400 roubles to be paid here and Yuri deals with that.

He takes us to the ferry office, inside the terminal building, so we can pay for our tickets and the bike's freight. There is a small hiccup. For the second time they've noticed the bike is registered in a company name and may not be permitted to land. That's overcome with a phone call to Korea. We can take the bike!

Next stop is the customs office. I don't think we would have even found the building without Yuri. It's in the middle of the city, at the end of a narrow street. There's no parking available and we have to walk along a couple of laneways to get to it.

Inside there are about 20 truck drivers milling around. Yuri walks past them, through a closed door and into an office where a man in a uniform with plenty of brass and medals is sitting behind a huge desk. They exchange pleasantries, our paperwork is stamped and we head back into the crowd. Yuri knocks on a closed sliding window and it's opened by a young attractive woman with long, painted nails who doesn't seem to mind that he has interrupted her morning tea break. She stamps our papers and it's done. Yuri obviously gets special treatment here. Back in the outer office the truck drivers are still milling around, waiting with their paperwork.

It's been nearly three months since we crossed into Russia from Helsinki and here we are in Vladivostok, on the other side of the world's largest country, getting ready to head home.

Shirley: Back at the hotel, Christian and Mike invite us to join them on a tour of the city. This proves to be the perfect way to see the most of this city before we bid a fond farewell to Mother Russia.

There's plenty of things I don't know about Vladivostok. Actor Yul Brynner was born here and his family home overlooks the port. Controversial author of *The Gulag Archipelago* Russian writer, Aleksandr Solzhenitsyn is commemorated with a very impressive statue on the waterfront. After living outside of Russia in exile since 1974 he returned to his homeland in 1994, arriving in Vladivostok.

When Vlad was the home of the Soviet's Pacific submarine fleet the city was closed to all outsiders – foreign and Russian. Stalin made it clear foreigners were unwelcome by murdering many and deporting the rest.

Today more than 40,000 students attend the university that was closed by Stalin in the 1930s and reopened by Khrushchev in the 1950s. The state-of-the-art campus is on Russky Island, at the end of a very striking suspension bridge.

The tour takes us to the old lighthouse that once guided the submarines home and to the S-56 submarine, now landlocked in front of the moving memorial to the city's war dead. Inside, the submarine has been left as it was during the war years — right down to the photo of Joseph Stalin, presumably in place to remind the sailors what they were fighting for.

•

After our tour we're all hungry and head out to a brewery restaurant recommended by Yuri. It's very cosmopolitan with scores of different beers brewed on the premises. The food is good and the conversation lively. We've all travelled a long way from home and have plenty of tales to share.

•

We board Eastern Dreaming about lunchtime and find our first class cabin. It's certainly not what we expected. It's listed as 'four berth' and the company couldn't tell us if we would be sharing. There are no bunks, just sleeping mats and quilts to lay out on the floor. Luckily we have the whole room to ourselves.

The duty-free shop has a fine bottle of wine that we use to toast what has been an amazing journey.

Our selfie skills are improving with a terrific shot of us with the Vladivostok sign behind us.

As we pull away from the dock, my last sight of Vladivostok is the statue of Lenin, peeping over the shipping terminal.

Goodbye Mother Russia. Goodbye Lenin. I believe we are both going to miss you.

South Korea

17 – 25 September

Brian: It has been a peaceful night on board the Eastern Dreaming sailing from Vladivostok to the South Korean port of Donghae. When we are getting close to port a crew member takes us to the car deck so we can load our gear onto the bike. Now it's just a matter of waiting for the crew to ready the ferry for disembarkation.

Passengers with bikes are told to wait on the back deck. As well as us, there are about 20 local bikers on board who have been to Russia for a short holiday. The men are all dressed in leathers with jackets covered in patches. Topped off with very dark wraparound sunglasses, they really look the part – born to be wild. They're members of a club and one, who speaks very good English, introduces us to the president. He's a very fit-looking man, probably younger than us. I'm gobsmacked when they tell us he's 70. I hope I'm that fit at the same age.

As we say goodbye one of the bikers tells me to be careful and not ride on the highways. What?

•

It takes us only a few minutes to clear through customs. In the terminal building we are met by an official from the shipping company. In his office we complete the paperwork for our temporary insurance. The insurance is a bit expensive, US$68 for just six days, but we have to register the bike for one year as well and that's going to set us back another US$240. We're only going to be in the country for a few days, but we have no option. I hand over the credit card.

As the paperwork is finalised I ask about restrictions.

'No restrictions. But you can't ride on tollways or major highways.' Surely that can't be right?

•

Our plan is to get to a hotel near the airport in Seoul where we'll leave some of our luggage and then ride south to Busan, the international port where the bike will be packed into a crate for the journey home.

I key the hotel's address into the GPS and we hit the road. We haven't gone far when we are directed on to a major road with a toll gate. The woman in the toll both is verging on hysterical.

'No. No. You must go back.'

Okay, so it is right. We cannot ride a motorcycle on a tollway.

'How do we get back?'

She directs us on to a slip road which takes us onto the other side of the same road, to another toll booth.

This woman is calmer and tells us to move over to one side. I try to explain we have come from the other side of the road and are trying to get off this tollway but she won't listen. She just keeps pointing to a small parking area.

Against my better judgment, I pull up and within a minute we are surrounded by more women. They are shrieking that we can't be here. One is taking photos of us and the bike.

Eventually they calm down and we ride away, not knowing if anything will come of the incident, now they have photos of the bike's registration plate. That was an experience.

Shirley: These women are crazy. Lots of shouting and gesticulating.

It's mid-afternoon now, but Seoul isn't that far. Reprogramming the GPS to avoid tollways we head off again.

The back roads are pretty good and the scenery quite lovely. We ride past rice paddies and small pastures with oxen grazing. There are snow-capped mountains on the horizon.

The traffic is really heavy and it's slow going. By the time we get close to the hotel it's dark. Neither of us likes riding at night, but we can't be that far from the hotel.

The next turn is a toll road, so we avoid that and try another road and then another. Despite the GPS settings, all roads are taking us back to that toll road.

Completely bamboozled and bloody tired we go onto the toll road hoping for some advice on how to get where we are going.

We are met with another shrill woman who directs us to a parking

On the road in South Korea

Fellow bikers, South Korea

Crating up, South Korea

area. A young man comes to talk to us. He tells us we can't be on this road. We know that. We'd just like some advice on how to get to our hotel.

Eventually he hands Brian his mobile phone to speak to his boss. The solution to our problem is easy. The man on the phone tells Brian to leave the bike here and get a taxi to the hotel.

We don't think so.

The young man gets in his car and escorts us down an emergency slip road and off the tollway.

•

Riding back towards central Seoul the traffic is horrendous even though it is now nearly 10 o'clock at night. We spot a neon 'motel' sign and I find the small motel at the top of a narrow, steep flight of stairs. The woman running the motel comes down to show Brian where he can park the bike, getting the chef at the restaurant next door to shift his car to make space.

We are both shattered and it's an effort to carry all of our gear up the stairs, but we don't feel we can leave anything on the bike here, on the street. Once inside the room we are presented with some fruit and juice. Enjoying the snack, we have time to take in our surroundings. The wall paper is pictures of women in skimpy shorts and wet T-shirts. The welcome pack includes condoms. It all seems a bit odd.

I hit the email and the mobile to ring the hotel to explain our predicament and change the booking for our room. They are surprised we couldn't get to the hotel but agree to change the booking without a penalty.

Showered, Brian gets into bed and asks, 'What should I do with this?'

He's holding up a bag of ropes he found beside the bed. Hmmm.

Brian: Similar to the beds we encountered in Vietnam last year, this one is as hard as a rock, but after the horrendous day we had yesterday nothing stopped me from getting a good night's sleep.

Right next door to the hotel is a French bakery with fresh sandwiches and pastries that make a pretty good breakfast.

•

It is another beautiful day and the countryside is picture perfect. In the fields, men and women in conical hats are picking vegetables. There are more rice paddies and cattle.

The roads are still very slow. I don't know that we'll make it to Busan tonight, even though it's less than 400 kilometres away.

At lunchtime we find a café in the bottom of an office block in a very modern area. Where is it? Can't say. Don't know.

We order the lunch special and ask that it not be too spicy. It's chicken and rice with a kimchi and some other side dishes. I'd hate to have a hot one. We both break out in a sweat.

•

As the afternoon wears on I know I'm not going to make it to Busan. I'm weary from the concentration levels needed to deal with the traffic. Over the rooftops I spot a 'Motel' sign and head for it.

It must be something about the difference between a hotel and a motel here. This establishment offers rooms for a few hours or overnight. The carpark is protected by a screen so passers-by can't see the cars. This is good security for the bike but I'm sure that's not what the owners have in mind.

We get another welcome kit, complete with condoms, a couple of toothbrushes and a comb.

Our room has a huge spa bath with a window so you can watch your companion bathe while you lie in the bed. There's no bag of ropes, though.

Shirley: Now, Busan is only a couple of hours' ride away so Brian suggests we check out the freight yard before we find our hotel. That way we'll know where we need to go the day after tomorrow to lodge the bike.

The address is confusing. Not only are the buildings and yards on the street numbered, the streets are numbered as well. We are looking for Sanmakgongdanuk 6-gil. We can find 5-gil and 7-gil, but not 6-gil. It must be here somewhere.

We are riding around aimlessly when I spy a truck making a delivery in a side street and get Brian to stop. We are looking for a freight yard, surely a truck driver will know where it is. He doesn't but a woman at the company he is delivering to gets me to come inside and searches the company and the address on the Internet. She has a lengthy conversation with an older man, presumably about our predicament.

When she can't find a map for me she tells me to come with her.

In the rush to explain what is going on to Brian, I leave my gloves on the back seat of the bike when I get into a car with the woman and her father. They are using their iPhone to find the address. Brian follows us on the bike. They have the same problem as us – the address is nowhere to be found. They have lengthy, animated discussions and then stop at a factory, at the top of a very steep hill, and ask the security guard. He has no idea either.

The woman apologises to me. In broken English she says the street is not here and the company is not here.

She has been so kind, driving me around for about 20 minutes, trying to find the mysterious yard.

I bid the couple farewell and go back to Brian and the bike. I ask him if he picked up my gloves off the back of the bike. He had no idea they were on the seat, so now I am down one pair of good summer gloves and I have a very unhappy husband.

After a terse conversation about wearing my winter gloves in this heat I get on and we're about to ride off when the car turns up again. The woman is waving madly for us to follow her. Not to be deterred, they continued looking after dropping me off and have found the freight yard. They lead us there and there is no doubt, it's the right place. Before we can thank them, they are driving off with a toot of their horn and a wave out the window.

You would think that 6-gil would be between 5-gil and 7-gil. No. It's near 13-gil. At last we now know where we need to head to crate the bike. Brian logs it into the GPS.

Determined to find my gloves, Brian backtracks to where we met our rescuers and there, in the middle of the road, they are. One has been run over but it has survived the experience.

•

Shops, restaurants, bars, karaoke and neon lights – Busan has them all but before we can wine and dine we have to get the bike clean. To get it back into Australia it has to be pristine to pass the quarantine checks.

Our hotel has an undercover carpark with a tap – the perfect place to wash the bike and get it clean enough to bring back to Australia.

It's a good plan, but when we mention it to the people on reception they tell us it is not permitted because the water will run down the street. We probably shouldn't have asked.

In the side street there is a grill over a drain. With an old bucket we purloined from a building site and cleaning liquid and cloths from the local convenience store we set to cleaning the bike, parking it over the grill so none of the excess water runs down the street. We don't want to upset the authorities.

We are right near the carpark for a local church. The men don't seem to be going to church but wait with their cars while the family goes, bring us food – cakes from the church service and pieces of fruit. I guess they are paying us for the enjoyment we are giving them for our street theatre performance.

Brian: To avoid the traffic, we head to the freight yard early. Even at 7am it is hectic on the streets of Busan. At least the GPS gets us right to the yard's gate without a hiccup.

The workers are expecting us and have copies of all the paperwork. For the next hour they measure the bike and build the crate around it. They are aware the wood has to be treated to pass the Australian quarantine standards and put the approved stamp on every face of the crate.

Paperwork signed, bike crated and we're in a taxi heading to the airport to collect the hire car to take us back to Seoul.

Now that we can use the toll roads and major highways it takes us about four hours to get to our airport hotel. I only need the hotel's phone number for the car's GPS to lock in the hotel's address. It's top-shelf technology. It then drives me crazy, telling me every 10 or 20 kilometres that driving can be dangerous and I must be careful.

The going was slow on the local roads but the scenery was magnificent. We don't see much on the toll roads. We stop at a service centre and find it's a major shopping complex with a Disney outlet and a golf shop, as well as the usual assortment of food stores.

Shirley: We are now one short plane trip from home. As a very special treat we are flying home business class. Sipping champagne, at the pointy end of the plane, sitting on a seat which will lay back to a bed when I get weary I get the feeling I was made for this kind of travel.

But with that in mind – I wouldn't change the past six months for anything. Even the hard days, the hot days, the cold days – they've all been a part of an amazing adventure.

- 36,300 kilometres
- 18 countries
- Scores of statues of Vladimir Lenin

Acknowledgements

Special thanks to Alan and Galia Hardy, Lorrae Willox and Russ Radcliffe for their help in putting this book together. Also Sonia Dewhurst who kept the home fires burning; freight agents Yuri Melnik, Wendy Choi and Dave Milligan from *Get Routed*; and Dylan Spence from *Flight Centre* who organised the best deal so Shirl could fly home sitting in the pointy end of the plane.

Roads are for journeys, not destinations

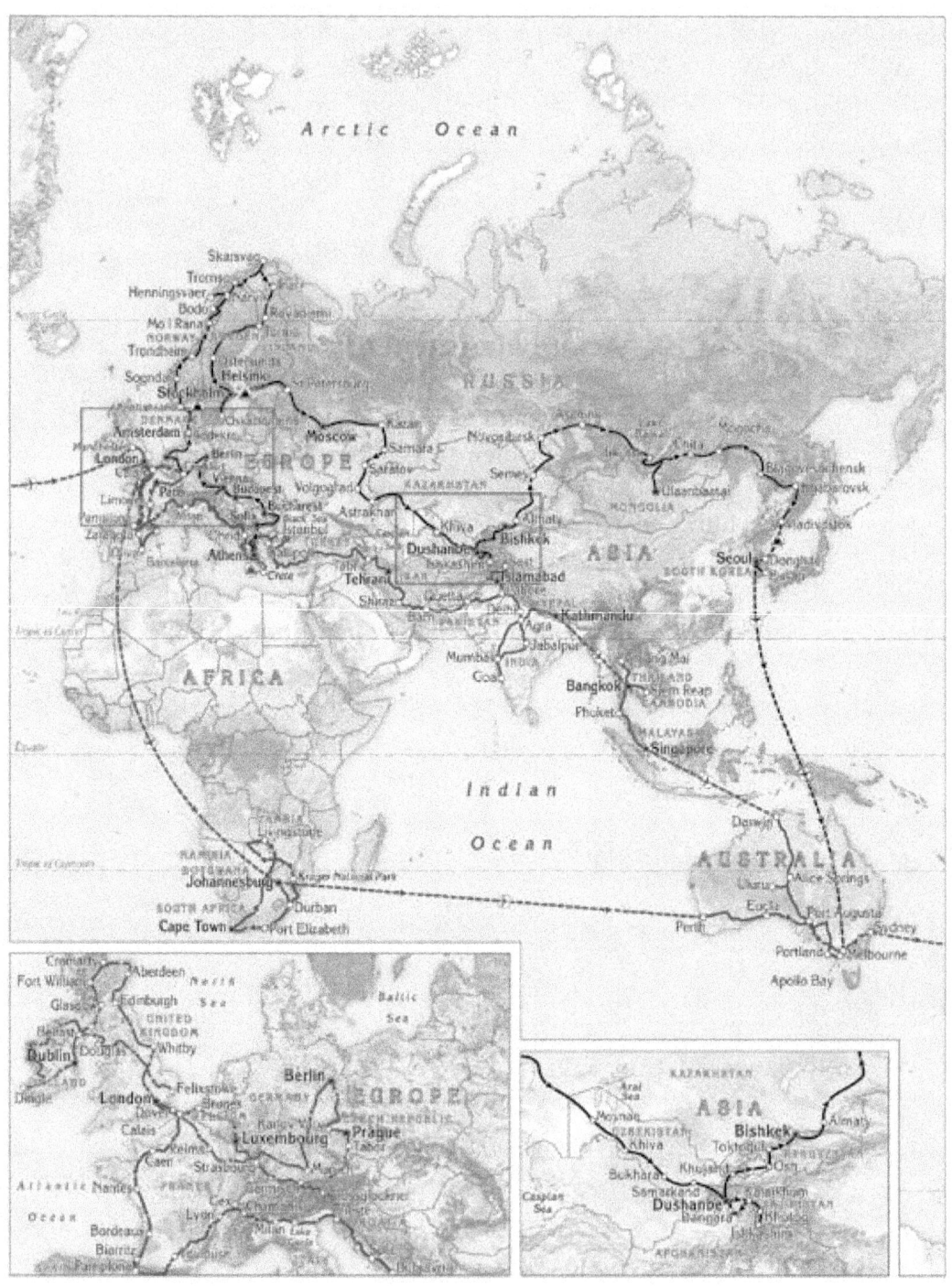

More than 175,000 kilometres

Follow our journeys

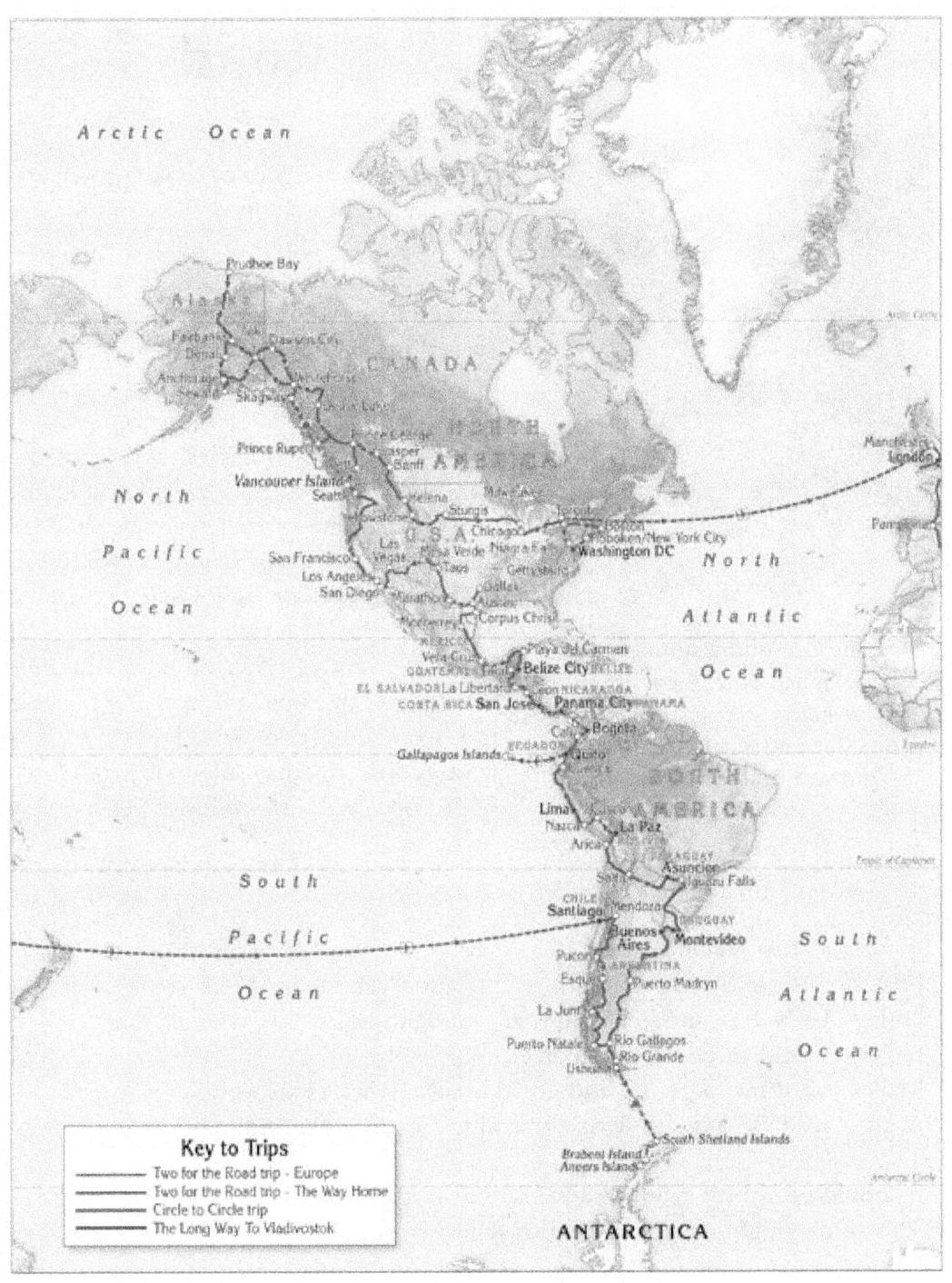

through 68 countries, over six continents

Two for the Road

Two for the Road is available direct from the authors - autographed on request - from *www.aussiesoverland.com.au* or as an eBook and paperback through online bookstores worldwide.

In 2003 Brian and Shirley took a grown up's 'gap year'. They shipped their motorcycle to England to fulfil a lifelong ambition of motorcycling across the world. In an incredible 350-day journey, they would do everything they'd ever dreamed of as well as getting much more than they bargained for.

Crossing 27 countries and covering 56,671 kilometres, they raced around the Isle of Man motorcycle circuit on Mad Sunday, survived Iran's traffic and travelled through Taliban strongholds under armed guard.

Shirley and Brian's story is an epic account of the ups and downs of seeing the world on two wheels – from the frustrations, to the splendour of some of Europe and Asia's most awe-inspiring sights.

Praise for *Two for the Road*
'Few Books are as inspirational as that just written by Melbourne journalist Shirley Hardy-Rix and her policeman husband Brian Rix.' *Herald Sun*
'For bikers and those with itchy feet.' *Sunday Age*
'Makes you want to get up and go.' *Australian Women's Weekly*
'A great read for anyone with a yearning for the open road and exotic climes,' *West Australian*
'It should be a must-read for adventurous hearts.' *Canberra Times*
'This book might tip undecided travellers over the edge – no bad thing.' *Two Wheels*

Circle to Circle

There were still many roads to ride, so when Brian Rix retired after 36 years as a police officer in Victoria and he and Shirley packed up their motorcycle and headed off for another adventure.

For the next 16 months, Brian and Shirley rode more than 82,000 kilometres through 32 countries on five continents.

They rode from the bottom of South America to the very top of North America – from the Antarctic Circle to the Arctic Circle. They rode over 5,000 metre mountain ranges, through snow and ice, through deserts and tropics, enduring altitude sickness and a near catastrophic breakdown in the heart of bear country.

Circle to Circle is an inspiring and engaging account of the travels of an adventurous couple. It will entertain you in your armchair, or it may even inspire you to get up and go.

Circle to Circle is available direct from the authors - autographed on request - from *www.aussiesoverland.com.au* or as an eBook and paperback through online bookstores worldwide.

Praise for *Circle to Circle*
'If you cannot take off on a journey yourself, the next best thing is to check out somebody else's travel album. It's amazing where a bike and an adventurous spirit can take a couple of retirees.' *The Age*
'You may not want to leap on a motorcycle after reading *Circle to Circle*, but you will want to travel.' *Herald Sun*
'*Circle to Circle* will entertain you and may even inspire you to explore some of the world.' *Australian Motorcycle News*

www.ingramcontent.com/pod-product-compliance
Lightning Source LLC
Chambersburg PA
CBHW070632160426
43194CB00009B/1440